GO TO HELL
AND MAKE
A U-TURN

GO TO HELL AND MAKE A U-TURN

REVISED EDITION

To Barbara,
Hope you enjoy our story
Marci Martin

Marci Martin

To order additional copies of this book, contact:
Xlibris Corporation
1-888-7-XLIBRIS
www.Xlibris.com
Orders@Xlibris.com

Contents

DEDICATED
TO YOU WHO HAVE OVERCOME
AND TO YOU WHO ARE STRUGGLING
YOU ARE NOT ALONE
YOU ARE LOVED
PRESS ON

AND TO OUR BELOVED GARY
FREE AT LAST

Chapter One

QUESTIONS, NO ANSWERS

I whirled around and cut out running. Someone yelled, "Hey, kid, stop!" and two guards were on my heels.

I felt like the last turkey in America on Thanksgiving. No place to hide and everyone wanted me. Thirteen-years-old and Casey Harper was on the run. I slammed smack into a sign that said Welcome to Tulsa Mall. Yeah, I was welcome all right.

When the guards grabbed me everything I had done that night flashed through my mind.

Shoplifting wasn't my idea. A guy at school made me do it. I called him Bully. He beat me up all the time and made a game of it, a game he called "punch". Every time I would piss him off he gave me a letter, the first time a "p", the second time a "u", and so on. It hurt, he hit hard, but it wasn't just the punches that hurt. Even then I felt I had no one to turn to. What could I have said anyway? Everyone at school thought the whole thing was a big joke. If I said anything, I'd be laughed at and known as a wimp. Bad enough being short and fat, but wimp is worse.

After I got the letters p-u-n-c Bully told me I had to steal some tapes that he needed instead of giving me the last punch. I guess he didn't want the game to be over as long as he could string me along and make me suffer. So a friend and I went to the mall to steal the tapes. Afterward, I called the friend Two-Face because that's what he turned out to be.

After we got to the mall we went into Kmart and took more than just the tapes. We got some film and a calculator, too. I took the tapes into the bathroom, ripped off the plastic wrapping, and shoved the tapes under my shirt. I had on a down jacket so no one could see what I had under it.

"Here," Two-Face said, handing me the film and calculator, "put these in there with the tapes."

So, then I had all the stuff on me.

Passing through the store, I noticed those little phones, you know, the ones that hang on the posts in the aisles. They rang as we walked by. The sales people answered, then stared at us. I got pretty nervous and knew something was way wrong, but kept going.

When I got to the front doors, I looked around and Two-Face was gone. A man ran by me out the doors, and then I saw Two-Face outside.

"Come on out here," Two-Face yelled, waving his arms. "I need to tell you something."

I was about to go to the cuckoo farm because I felt something was way out in left field. But being the intelligent kid that I was, I went on outside anyway.

"That man told me you were still inside and told me to get you out here," Two-Face said. His eyes looked scared, but he had a sneaky grin on his face.

Then I got the message. We couldn't get arrested until we stepped out the doors so the man wanted me outside with Two-Face, and Two-Face wasn't about to get arrested without me.

That's when I zipped up my jacket and took off running. The cold air stung my eyes. I knew I'd been screwed over by Two-

Face. Either he was born stupid or knew exactly what he was doing. I never found out which. If my vote counted I would have to vote for the born stupid theory.

Funny how I always ended up with the stupid ones. I found it hard to fit in with the regular kids because of the way I looked. It was easy to fit in with the rebel kids. They didn't expect anything of me. I didn't consider myself very smart anyway. All I had to do was drink and do drugs to fit in, and that came pretty easy. It was something I didn't have to work at. Maybe I was born stupid, too, because there I was, one guard holding my hands behind my back and the other one shouting questions at me. "Do you have anything that belongs to Kmart?" he barked.

"Nope," I said, being cool, I thought.

"What about the tapes, film, and calculator hidden under your shirt?" he said.

Well, my future looked dim and short at that point, especially knowing my dad would find out. That was all the punishment I needed, having to face Dad. I must have aged to twenty that night.

They took us back into the store. It was awful. Everybody stared at us. They processed us in a little office in the back of the store and called the police. Then it was time to call our parents.

"You have to make the call yourself, son," a lady security guard said. She was nice enough, tall and stringy, doing her job.

"No way in hell am I going to set up my own murder," was my reply. Two-Face and I started laughing. It was the kind of laugh that comes out and no matter how hard you try it keeps on coming.

"Why are you laughing?" she snapped at me.

"Don't be mad at us 'cause we might not live long enough to laugh again after our folks find out."

She smiled a little, but handed the phone to me anyway. It was my turn to make the call to my folks. I started to dial the number. "Please don't make me do this," I begged. I dragged out the dialing as long as I could, begging with her all the while.

-MART

The phone began to ring. One, two, three. I'll never forget those three rings. In between rings I found myself pleading with God, I mean really pleading, to let my mom, not Dad, answer the phone. I guess my prayer was answered because I heard Mom saying, "Hello."

After I said the word "shoplifting", she repeated it so loud I knew Dad would hear. He'd be sitting close by watching TV like he did every night. I heard his recliner swing shut faster than I'd ever heard it before and I knew he was on his feet. When I heard that terrible screeching noise, I handed the phone over to the guard.

Soon I'd have to face my dad. My life might as well be over.

* * *

SUB CHAPTER ONE

"Mom . . . uh . . . uh . . . I've been arrested for shoplifting."

"What? Shoplifting?" My voice turned shrill. Was I asleep having a nightmare?

Another voice on the phone startled me, and I had to make myself listen. The man had a deep, stern, unfeeling tone, sounding routine, like what did he care that he was talking about my son.

"Are you Anne Harper? Got a son named Casey? Yes, ma'am, shoplifting. Him and another boy. Picked them up around seven o'clock tonight at the mall down on Memorial Drive. You'll have to come get him. Precinct downtown, 600 Tulsa Civic Center."

I wheeled away from the phone and stared at Ted. "You heard?"

His face had a look of bewilderment and disgust, a not uncommon look where our son was concerned. His square jaws tightened and I knew he was grinding his teeth.

"Dumb, just downright dumb!" he snapped. "Maybe we should let him cool his heels a while. Might teach him a lesson."

He was up out of his chair, fishing for his car keys, so I knew he didn't mean it. I was too confused, angry, and scared to know what to say right then, so I kept quiet.

While we were getting our coats out of the hall closet, Gina came out of her room, a history book in her hand. "Where are you going?" she asked, yawning.

We both jumped when Ted slammed the closet door.

"It's your brother," I answered, trying to hold back the tears. "He's been arrested for shoplifting, and we have to go downtown and get him."

"Shoplifting?" Her voice was about as shrill as mine was at the mention of that word. Her green eyes widened as she frowned. "Can I go with you?"

"No, honey, stay here. Shouldn't take too long."

Ted rattled his car keys, impatient to leave. And our little West Highland terriers, Angel and Muffett, milled around our feet like they knew something was wrong. I reached down and petted Angel. Her soft fur felt comforting and her round black eyes looked into mine. Such trusting love, I thought.

The minute I got in the car, tears poured.

Finally, when I could manage to speak, I said, "Why in the world is he stealing? He has about everything he wants. Maybe the other boy made him do it. I'll pinch his little head off, that's what I'll do." Crying gave way to anger, and a little nagging voice told me to be calm when I saw Casey. Ted's quick temper might make an already bad situation worse. I wondered if Ted's stomach was churning like mine.

His silence worried me. I visualized a grenade with the pin removed ready to explode. I glanced over at him. His light brown hair was uncombed. Neither of us had taken time to do anything to ourselves before we left home.

For once in my life it wasn't important. He turned his head quickly, and, for an instant, I saw the desperation in his sharp blue eyes.

"Who was the other boy?" he asked, turning back to watch the traffic ahead.

"A new boy at school named Danny. All I know is his parents are divorced. I've never met him. Should've checked him out first, but how could I have known this would happen?" I took a tissue from my purse, wiped my eyes and blew my nose. "Casey asked to go over to Danny's house for a little while tonight and since it's Saturday I thought it was OK. He lives on 56th, a few streets over from here."

We drove on in silence. A gentle rain began to fall. The rhythmic swishing of the windshield wipers broke the stillness. Trees and houses blurred past the windows. I watched the raindrops slide across the glass while I sank into my thoughts. Somewhere in my notions about raising children, I supposed teenage years to be the best—a golden time when children learned responsibility and glimpsed their potential in the world. Gina, at seventeen, with her dark hair and sparkling green eyes, was quiet and happy within herself. But thirteen-year-old Casey, blond and fair, always seemed to be struggling with something.

Maybe it bothered him that most of his friends were taller. One time he looked at me with droopy eyes and said, "Do you think I'll be this short, like you, when I'm thirty?"

"I'll bet you'll be just perfect," I said. Then I reminded him his dad grew taller after he graduated from high school. I hoped that would comfort him, but he turned away and switched on the TV.

Neither one of our children had ever been in any kind of serious trouble before. Casey had some problems in school; being the class clown kept him in hot water with his teachers. A hyper-active child, it was hard for him to settle down to anything. He was good at sports, well-coordinated, and had a natural musical talent. Anything that came easy he sloughed aside, never giving himself credit for being good at anything, although he was quick-witted and quick to learn anything he put his mind to. His teachers told me he often finished class work ahead of some of the class, then he figured it was play time. But why, why this? I shuddered, imagining how scared he probably was waiting for us to come.

"What are you thinking about," I heard Ted ask. "You're a long way off." He reached over and squeezed my hand.

"Thinking about our kids. All the things we've done— music lessons, Scouts, sports—didn't they mean anything? And the vacations we've had together. We've had fun, haven't we? I thought keeping them busy would keep them out of trouble. I've always heard that."

"Ever wonder if adopting was the right thing for us to do?"

"No, I've never doubted. From the very first time I held each one of them, you remember how I felt, I knew they were our own. It was hard to realize I hadn't given birth to them. Have you ever . . . ?"

"Never doubted either. I just wondered if maybe we were too old to understand the times. Kids into drugs and drinking. It's another world now."

We lapsed into silence again. The rain stopped and Ted switched off the wipers.

I wondered if, like me, all adoptive parents feel they have to prove to the world how worthy they are to have children entrusted to them. Maybe I tried too hard.

Stepping out of the car at the precinct, the cold wind cut through me. On our way into the tall grey building I buttoned my coat and stayed close to Ted, whose tall frame shielded me from the wind. The air smelled fresh and clean. I wished *I* could feel fresh and clean.

We asked for the juvenile division and took the elevator to the third floor. The elevator door opened to a large room with a desk at one end near the door and folding chairs lined up against the far wall. The pale green walls and faded linoleum floor were as depressing as the scene before me. The place was full of people. Some of the men were yelling at their children. Mothers were either looking on in stunned silence or crying. A few were yelling back at whomever was standing next to them. The smell of overheated bodies and stale cigarette smoke made my oversensitive nose twitch.

Strange, I thought. Tulsa had seemed such a quiet peaceful place to live. These were things I read about in the newspaper or watched on television. Never imagined my family being involved in such a scene.

I saw a woman sitting by herself, and for some reason, I went over and asked, "Are you Danny's mother?" Out of all the women in the room I don't know why I supposed she was. She nodded her head and burst into tears. I was suddenly thrust into the role of comforter for her, and this was good because I didn't have time to think about the rest of us. After a while she calmed down, and we waited.

Ted paced the floor. I couldn't help comparing him to the other men around me. He was by far the best looking of them all: tall, trim, and broad shouldered. His square jaws and the cleft in his chin reminded me of my older brother who was killed in the second world war. The Ted most people knew was not the man I knew. He had a tenderness seldom seen by others. His honesty and strength were my rock to lean on.

Wide double doors across the room suddenly squeaked open and two boys came toward us, heads down, dragging their feet. Danny's mother grabbed his hand and yanked him over to the deputy's desk. She didn't even bother to say thank you or goodbye to me. Oh well, I mused, I'll probably never see her again anyway.

Casey ducked his head. Sobs shook his broad chest. A short potbellied deputy marched over to us and said, "You'll have to report to Juvenile Hall in two weeks for a hearing." He laid his huge hand on Casey's shoulder, adding, "Better stay out of trouble, son, or they'll send you there to live." A frightening prospect, as if things weren't bad enough.

By the time we returned to our car, rain was falling again. Thunder rumbled in the distance.

"OK, Casey, what do you have to say about this mess you're in?" Ted said in a flat, controlled voice, staring at the streaks of light in front of the car.

Casey raised his head and peered up at me from the back seat. His eyes, the color of cornflowers, were shiny from tears, and his cheeks were damp and flushed. The dejection in his round face broke my heart. I was torn between wanting to take him in my arms and comfort him or shake some answers out of him.

He brushed tousled hair out of his eyes. The words rushed out like a soda pop exploding. "We were over at Danny's house and didn't have anything to do and he wanted to go to the mall . . . his mother wasn't home so we went . . . and Danny said, 'Let's take something, everybody does it' . . . so he took a calculator and I took some tapes . . . it was so easy he took something else . . . I took some film . . . we thought we'd better get outa there so we left and two guys came runnin' after us and pulled us back into the store and up into an office . . . they made me call you . . . then took us down to the jail." He gasped to catch his breath, was silent for a minute while we waited, then added quietly, "I'm sorry. I'll never do it again."

"You bet you won't if you know what's good for you," Ted threatened.

I couldn't speak at all. No one said a word the rest of the way home.

Gina opened the back door as the car pulled into the garage. Her eyes were wide and questioning. It was strange that no one said anything. We went inside, hung up our coats, and Ted slammed the closet door again. Would the grenade explode now, I wondered?

Casey went straight to his room, we followed close behind. He sat down on the far side of his twin bed, like he might have thought the distance would protect him from us.

Ted marched in and sat across from him. "I want answers," he snapped. "What in the world were you thinking about? Guess that's just it, you weren't thinking."

"Dad . . . "

"I don't want to hear any excuses from you. Reasons, maybe, but not excuses. There is never any excuse for stealing."

Casey sat on the side of his bed saying nothing, twisting a tissue in his hands until some pieces fell to the floor.

I leaned against the door frame listening, and Gina stood next to me holding my hand, waiting to talk to her brother.

"Casey," I said, "Can't you tell us any other reason you did it? You must have known it was wrong. Talk to us."

He didn't answer.

Ted shook his head in disgust. "You're grounded for a month. You're lucky I'm not grounding you forever." He got up and stormed out of the room.

My son looked like a crushed moth and I stood there staring, wanting to fuss at him and comfort him all at the same time, like I usually did when he was in trouble. I wished Ted could be like the father in the old TV show, "Father Knows Best", always calm, understanding, offering sage advice and solutions. The problem was that Ted and

Casey were too much alike, quick acting and quick tempered, overly sensitive.

"Better go to bed, both of you. We'll talk tomorrow," I said, because I was worn out trying to figure out what else to do.

Thunder rumbled overhead and rain beat against the windows. I thought, even the skies are angry tonight.

* * *

Chapter Two

ROLLER COASTER RIDE

AFTER the shoplifting incident more disturbing things followed, no more shoplifting, as far as we knew, but trouble in school and a growing indifference and distance on Casey's part. Ted and I thought that keeping him occupied would make a difference. He took trumpet lessons and played in the junior high band. Football, baseball, and soccer after school took off excess weight and he grew taller, though still short for his age. He sang in the Tulsa Boy's Choir until his voice changed.

After entering high school he dropped out of all activities. No more sports or music. And his grades dropped to a new low. He got a job working as a bus boy in a near-by restaurant and we heartily approved, thinking it would teach him responsibility. He wanted a car and contributed toward the purchase of an old Chevrolet.

One of the worst nights I recall was late one Saturday. Ted and I heard a loud bump in front of the house.

Ted hurriedly opened the door and said with disgust, "It's Casey. The car's up over the curb."

I rushed to see and, by that time, Casey was struggling to get out of the car. We couldn't believe our eyes, watching our son stumble toward the house.

"Are you going to leave the car like that?"

Casey didn't answer his father. He rushed into the bathroom and threw up. I gagged, listening to him, while Ted paced outside the bathroom door. When Casey came out, Ted followed him to his bedroom and watched in silent horror as Casey tried to take off his shoes and socks.

"He's so drunk he can't even take off his shoes," he said to me. Turning down the hall, he went into our bedroom and slammed the door. "I can't watch this anymore," I heard him say.

If I live to be a hundred, I'll never forget the anguish in his voice and his sad eyes.

And to make matters worse, later on that night a friend of Casey's crashed into Casey's car at the curb and wrecked a rear bumper.

I had heard other mother's say they couldn't do anything with their children and thought it ridiculous that they were so inept. Yet here we were with the same problem. When did we lose control, we wondered?

And how?

Casey's temperament had always been erratic, with mood swings and fits of temper. These were common characteristics of someone on drugs, we later learned. And yet, how would we have known he was into drugs at that time? Information about drugs was not prevalent in the 60's, 70's, and early 80's.

A sudden decline in the real estate market impelled us to consider moving to another state. My mother and brother lived in San Francisco, and Ted and I had often talked about living there someday.

We told our children we were going on a short vaca-
tion, didn't tell them the real reason because we weren't
certain about moving. It was an "exploratory" trip. Gina
was out of school and working, and we felt all right about
leaving them at home for a week or so. It was Casey's senior year and it had been a while since we'd had any trouble
with him.

Instead of going to San Francisco, we decided to see
about the possibilities in San Diego. We felt the climate
there would appeal to us more than the colder San Francisco weather.

Right away, we found San Diego to be all we had hoped
for. The climate was perfect, and the real estate market
was on the upswing. We spent one day with a business contact who offered Ted a place with his company. Our decision to move there was easily made.

When we called the children to tell them we were on
our way home, both were sobbing. One of our little terriers, Angel, had died quite suddenly that morning. We all
cried together and said a sad goodbye.

We arrived back home on a Saturday and broke the
news about moving. Gina took the news in stride, deciding to stay in Tulsa. Casey, on the other hand, threw a tan-
trum, refusing to leave his friends.

"Don't get so upset, son. We have to sell the house first.
That could take a while, so you'll have time to get used to
the idea. Besides, think about swimming in the ocean and
those tan California girls," his father said. He stood behind Casey, his hands on Casey's shoulders, playfully rock-
ing him back and forth.

Casey pulled away saying, "But I've gone to school here
since first grade . . . "

"We'll all make new friends," Ted countered, trying to
put the discussion to rest. Casey silently retreated to his
room.

The following Monday morning Ted listed our house with his company. A few days later one of his fellow agents showed the house to a young family. I stood aside watching them inspect this home I had loved, with its soft antique white walls and French blue carpets. The young family loved it, too, and signed the sales contract the next day. They wanted possession in thirty days.

We felt like we were caught in a whirlwind. Too fast, we thought, much too fast, but Ted agreed to the thirty day possession rather than lose the sale. Naturally, our plans had to be revised for this hurry-up move.

Sunday dinner seemed like a perfect time for a family conference. I plied them with fried chicken, one of our favorites, thinking maybe a good dinner would set the stage for what Ted and I had to say. I finished putting dinner on the dining room table and we all sat down.

While dishes of food were passed around, Ted plunged right in with the news about the house being sold.

"Looks like we'll have to move sooner than expected," he began.

"Wow, that was quick. Just listed it last week, didn't you?" Gina asked with a startled expression. "What about your work?"

"Job is already waiting for me. I'll go on to California and start studying for my real estate license, then come back next month for your mom. Meanwhile, some decisions need to be made."

"Like, what about me and school?" Casey asked with a cocky little smile.

"You'll have to stay here with Gina a few months until school is out. Dad will come back for you in June," I said, sipping iced tea. I tried to sound matter-of-fact and confident, but my heart began to pound.

"Why can't I just stay here until my senior year is over, too?"

"Leave you here another year? We couldn't stand to be away from you that long, honey," I said. That frightening thought made me gasp, like the air had been knocked out of me.

"You belong with us, Casey. Besides, you'll like San Diego. So many things to do. We can learn to surf." Ted raised his eyebrows and grinned at Casey. He made it sound so easy. "How about it, son, think you can get along OK staying with Gina? Of course, we'll have to find you both a place to live."

"It'll be fun on our own," Casey said, drumming his fingers on the table.

Gina wasn't amused. She waggled a finger at her brother and said, "You'll have to keep up your homework and stay out of trouble if you live with me." No doubt about the tone of her voice. She meant business.

Casey leaned back on the hind legs of his chair and quipped, "I can do that."

"How many times have I told you not to lean your chair back," I snapped at him. Thinking he was a bit too eager about the whole thing, I added, "This isn't all fun and games, Casey. Gina will be in charge. You'll have to keep that in mind. Anyway, it's only two months until school is out, and we don't want you to miss the end of this year with your buddies, so we have no choice, I guess. It seems foolish to take you out before the semester ends."

Except for her one remark, Gina was quiet through the discussion. I kept looking at her to see if I could tell what she was thinking. "We can start looking for an apartment tomorrow," I said to her. Finally, she pushed back her chair, stood up, and took some dishes to the kitchen.

"Are you OK with all this, honey?" I said following her. "We'll send you money for Casey's expenses. Is that what's on your mind?"

"No, that's not it. I'll enjoy having my own place again. I just don't want Casey to do anything crazy. You know how he is, always has to have his own way. These past few years haven't been easy on you guys."

Ted and Casey came strolling into the kitchen, bringing dirty dishes. "If we all work together it'll work out," Ted said in a way that seemed to put the whole discussion at an end.

Ted went on to San Diego and took his real estate course. He found a house in Encinitas, about twenty five miles north of San Diego. Then he flew back home to help me pack for the journey.

Early, the morning of March twenty-seventh, 1982, we kissed and hugged our children, loaded ourselves and our little terrier, Muffett, into the cab of the U-Haul truck, and waved a teary goodbye. Looking back through the window at our children, I thought how young they looked, how troubled, and wondered if we were doing the right thing. I missed them already and felt torn between being with my husband on this new venture and leaving my children in an uncertain situation.

We had no qualms about leaving Gina behind. She had a good job, with an innate sense of responsibility, who relished her independence. I knew she could take care of herself. Her ability to manage her little brother was what worried us. It was a time when we simply had to trust both of them to act responsibly, and know the move cross-country was the right thing for us to do. I knew I wouldn't relax until June when Ted could go back to Tulsa and bring Casey home to Encinitas. Leaving them behind was the hardest thing I ever had to do.

I gathered Muffett up in my arms and hugged her. I had to hold on to something warm right then.

During the months that followed, we kept in close touch by telephone. Gina's main problem with Casey was making him keep her house clean. He always left a mess in the kitchen, she complained.

"So, what's new about that?" I replied. Other than that, we didn't know about any more problems between them.

We both loved our new home. Ted was busy getting settled in his new job while I explored our new surroundings. Our house was three miles from the beach and every day I strolled along the shore, picking up shells, kicking my feet through the cool sand, and praying for my family. For a girl from Texas, this was heaven. Many afternoons when Ted finished work, we took our dinner to the beach.

New sights and smells filled my senses: girls in bikinis, naked children playing in the sand, surfers and boogie boarders skimming over foaming waves, and once in a while I'd spot dolphins jumping through the water. Odors of sea weed and fish and coconut suntan lotion tickled my nose.

June finally rolled around, and Ted flew back to Tulsa for Casey. When they arrived home, I couldn't believe my eyes. Casey had grown about two inches taller and was slimmer. How could he have grown so fast? His hair was long and unkempt, and all his jeans had holes in them. He looked and acted like a different person. Soon he let us know just how very different he was.

We found out right away how he felt about the move. He was still angry and resentful about leaving the friends he'd grown up with. We didn't blame him, but we expected him to adjust sooner than he was willing to. He didn't try to hide his feelings and was impossible to get along with most of the time.

He moped around the house for weeks, ending up with a fever and upset stomach.

One day I'd had enough and went into the living room where he was watching television. "Are you going to spend your life sitting on this floor in front of the TV?"

"Aw, come on, Mom, move . . . I can't see."

"Well, I'll fix that," I said, turning the TV off. I sat down on the sofa behind him. "Casey, lying around this house won't move you back to Tulsa or change anything. You've got to get on with your life. School doesn't start for two more months. You could get a job and keep busy, maybe meet some new people."

He said nothing, frowned, turned over on his stomach, and buried his head in a pillow.

"How about it, honey? I don't like seeing you so unhappy," I said, fingering his hair. A little verbal compassion might work, I hoped.

"OK, Mom. I'll see about a job tomorrow." he mumbled into the pillow.

Soon he went to work at a restaurant washing dishes for the rest of the summer, and was strangely cooperative. In September he began his senior year, and quickly found his school to be very different than the Tulsa schools. Most of the kids wore shorts, and some of the girls wore halter tops. After checking attendance each morning, seeing empty seats, Casey said the teachers would remark, "Surf must be up," and made little of it. Casey seemed to settle down, at least for a short time, meeting new friends, and still working on weekends.

One night he went to a party and met a girl. "What a fox, Mom. She was with another guy, but I decided I had to go out with her." He grinned in a way I'd never seen before.

Karen was her name. He brought her home one day to meet me and I wondered what in the world he saw in her. I guess I'd expected some raving beauty. She was pretty all right, tall, about eye-to-eye with Casey, and extremely thin. She was wearing what turned out to be her constant mode of dress: tight-fitting pants or jeans and a baggy shirt that looked like it was two sizes too large for her. Everything she wore was a drab color. Long light brown hair curled loosely around her shoulders, and she wore no make-up. One thing, though, she had large shiny brown eyes that were quite striking, yet secretive.

Her manner was restless, like Casey. When they were at the house, they would turn on the TV or stereo for a short time, going in and out of the front door, never settling down. It was impossible to carry on any kind of continuing conversation. This annoyed and disturbed me a great deal.

One morning at breakfast Ted said, "Tell us about Karen, where she lives, and about her folks."

Casey pushed away the rest of his cereal. "Dan and Jo are their names. They live in Solana Beach. Nice house. Karen's older brother lives in Colorado somewhere, and Joyce, her sister, is in a drug rehab center down in San Diego. The brother is an addict, too."

Ted's eyes met mine. "Karen too?" Ted asked.

Casey was on his feet shoving his chair up to the table. "I don't know, Dad," he snapped. "Gotta go."

He and Karen spent every cent he earned, and we were afraid the money was going for drugs. His behavior lapsed back into the old routine. We tried everything we knew to reach him, but nothing worked.

He graduated from high school early, in January, instead of June, and got a job at a service station not far from home. Going to college was out of the question as far as he was concerned.

The boys he brought home were a scroungy looking group, and Casey didn't look much better. His hair was long and uncombed, and his clothes always looked like they'd been slept in. Grease-stained hands and fingernails were part of his usual look, too. I didn't feel like I could trust most of his friends to be there alone, so I tried to keep a sharp eye on them without being too obvious to Casey.

One afternoon he brought a ragged looking fellow

home with him. Taking me aside for a minute he whispered, "Charlie's out of a job , no place to stay, been in jail a while. Can he stay here a few days until he finds a place?"

"Been in jail? What for?" The thought of this guy living in my home made me shiver.

"Oh, I don't know, Mom. Drinking, I think."

"No, Casey, no. I don't want him here. I'm sorry, but that's how I feel."

He turned away with a disgusted grunt, called out to Charlie, and left the house. He didn't return until late that night.

He knew better than to bring liquor into the house, but many times I could smell it on his breath. I always hated that smell, reminded me of my dad.

He came home drunk more than once. I thought Ted would blow up, he was so angry. "One more time and you're out of here," he threatened.

"I won't do it again," Casey promised each time, looking sincere.

"And one more thing. Don't bring any more of the guys from work here again."

"What's the matter with them?" Casey snarled.

"Your mother says she doesn't like them hanging around."

Casey shot a look at me.

"I don't trust that one guy . . . you know, the one you said had been in jail," I said, defending myself. Why did Ted put me in this position anyway, I wondered. It would be nice sometime to be able to have a normal conversation between us. But Ted was always threatening or laying down the law while Casey bristled, leaving me in the proverbial middle, trying to pull them together.

Casey muttered something and left the house. His reaction to trouble was to run away, as if that was the answer.

Not long after that, Casey moved out, hellbent to go

his own way. He lived in his car or with friends. Occasionally, he came home for a short while. He'd do his laundry
and play the piano for hours, then leave.

It was terrible each time he left, never knowing where
he was going. One time Ted said, "I'm not letting him in
here again. I'm better off not knowing what he's up to."

"Maybe you can shut him out, but I can't. I simply can
not do that," I replied, and my throat tightened. It was unusual
for me to buck Ted, but this time I had to make myself heard.
It would never be possible for me to shut Casey out of our
lives. I was afraid Ted would follow through with his threat,
yet, the next time Casey came home, he said nothing, knowing
how I felt.

It seemed to me that I was always caught between Ted
and Casey, trying to keep the peace. This infuriated Ted, but
I couldn't stand the arguments and yelling. My role was precarious at best, keeping Casey's actions to myself to avoid a
scene. Not a smart move on my part, as it turned out, but it
was the role I chose to play, right or wrong.

As time passed, Ted grew more and more reluctant to
talk about Casey. I suppose the only way he could deal with it
was to try to shut Casey out of his life. But he cared deeply,
no denying that. It was a shame Casey didn't know this for
himself. Casey came home one day and we had an argument,
I don't recall what about, yet I do remember telling him as
emphatically as I could muster, "I love you with all my heart,
but I don't like what you're doing with your life right now." I
put my hands on his shoulders and tried to search out his
eyes. "Somewhere deep inside you there's a good guy just
waiting to get out. If you ever get in touch with him, you'll
probably find whatever it is you're looking for."

He gazed at me with a blank expression, like he had
no idea what I meant. I hugged him. One thing I could
count on from Casey was a big hug. The sweetness in him
was always there and never changed.

Every time he left home I felt empty like I might never see him again. My heart ached watching him drive away that day: my child that could exasperate, confuse, delight, or tease with a word, a tilt of his tousled head, or shuffling step; this boy with hands never clean, always taking things apart, never to put them back again; this boy who, when asleep, made me weep with love and worry for his troubled and troubling ways. I remembered him as an infant, too stubborn even then. I would pat his little back trying to coax out a burp, but he held it in until he'd explode, spewing milk all over us. Then he'd flash his sweet innocent smile, like he'd won. I think I knew even then what lay ahead. What makes him this way, I questioned, and what can I do to set things right?

Somewhere I read that children inherit addictions from parents, and since Casey was adopted, this could have been true. But Ted and I chose not to believe this theory. Our religious convictions discounted this entirely, since we believe we are all children of God. We felt that we should be responsible for his character, not someone else.

Drug and alcohol addictions were subjects Ted and I knew nothing about, being non-smokers and non-drinkers.

The *why* of it puzzled me—why a person succumbed to that kind of potentially fatal self-destruction.

Casey was loved, never physically or verbally abused. We did things together as a family, had dinner at the same table each night, went to church on Sundays, and cared equally about our children. For some reason, Casey was insecure, having little self-confidence, and he held the notion that we favored Gina over him. Our reassurances failed to change this misconception, no matter how hard we tried.

A human answer never came. I finally accepted his determination to go his own way, wherever it took him. My only course was to pray and know that God was watching over him and would guide him in a way that he could understand. Brave words. I attempted to maintain this attitude, but some nights I would waken suddenly and break out in a cold sweat.

Karen had dropped out of school months before they met, and this worried Casey. One night after dinner, she started clearing the table and Casey followed her to the kitchen.

"How about going to that special school you mentioned. I'll help you get your diploma," he said.

"I don't like school, you know that," she replied, banging dishes around in the sink. Casey had told us she dropped out of school because she couldn't cope with any kind of pressure.

"I'll do that," I said, trying to save my dishes from destruction. The annoyed look on her face surprised me. She should have been grateful that Casey wanted to help her.

"Can't get a decent job without a high school diploma, Karen. I'll help you with homework if that's what you're worried about."

Ted appeared in the doorway, taking in the whole scene. I was certain his thoughts were the same as mine. When did Casey ever do his *own* homework?

Karen was quiet a minute, then she glanced over at Casey. "OK," she said. "I'll do it."

Ted and I exchanged looks. We were proud of Casey for his influence with Karen, but surprised at his attitude. After all, this was the same boy who had shown such nonchalance about his own schooling. After this happened, I knew he really cared about Karen. I was not happy about it, not one little bit.

One spring day in 1983 I had a telephone call from Gina. "What would you think about me moving out there and going to college? Could I live at home again?"

"I don't believe my ears! You want to go to college? The girl who said she never wanted to see school again?"

"It's the only way to get a better job, Mom. I know that now. Would it be OK?"

"Sounds like a great plan to me," I said. It was impossible to hide my delight.

Later that summer we rented a car and drove back to Tulsa to help her move. We packed her belongings in a small U-Haul truck which Ted drove, while I traveled with Gina and her pit bull dog, Suzy, in Gina's Ford.

It was fun having my daughter home again. Her calm, easy-going manner was quite a change from Casey. We'd always been close, and I hoped she could shed some light about her brother.

"What's going on with Casey?" I'd ask time after time. She would shrug her shoulders. "I don't know, Mom. He doesn't tell me much."

I was certain she knew more than she would tell and suspected she kept it to herself out of loyalty to her little brother.

Casey finally left the service station and found a better job at a solar company. This led to another job with a computer manufacturer. He came over after work one day and asked his dad, "How about helping me buy a new car? The old Chevy's in pretty bad shape."

Ted sat down at the kitchen table, picked up a pad and pencil, and started doodling with figures. "Tell you what I'll do. If you'll go to college I'll pay for it. Tuition here is better than anywhere else. Rather see you do that than work yourself silly at some job with no future."

"Aw, Dad, I don't want to go to school. You should know that. Besides, who says my job has no future?" He stood before his dad, shifting his weight impatiently, hands on his hips. He looked defensive and angry.

"Don't get all riled up, Casey. Just thought I'd offer you something better than what you're doing, that's all."

"I'm happy with what I'm doing. What I really want is a better car. Will you help me get one or not?"

"What kind do you have in mind?" Ted asked.

Stubbornness was a characteristic Casey wore like armor. I wondered what would happen if Ted ever said no and really meant it. I always found it hard to say no to him myself. How could we be so wishy-washy?

"What I want is a Camaro."

"You're talking big bucks, even for a used one. I'll see what I can do. What monthly payments can you afford?"

At that point I left the room. Wrangling over money was not my cup of tea, and I didn't want to hear any more. I'd let them fight it out by themselves.

Ted found out he could lease a 1983 Camaro. It seemed the best deal he could make at the time, and Casey agreed to make the payments. Inside I screamed, "Don't do it!" but I kept quiet as usual. And, as I feared, the deal went sour.

After a while Casey began skipping payments, and Ted had to rant and rave for the money. Finally, after about a year and a half, Ted took the car away from him and I had to drive it.

There are two things I really hate: boiled cabbage and having to drive that car. I was given no other option, though. The car became mine to have and to hold. My five-year-old Ford Granada was paid for, and we let Casey take it for smaller payments. But he wrecked it by the end of the first week he had it.

I don't think I've ever seen Ted angrier than when he saw that car. I couldn't believe it, either. My trusty old car, without a scratch on it the week before, looked like a hare-lipped monster.

"He'd better not *ever* ask me for anything again," Ted raved. "I've had enough."

Sure, sure, I complained silently. Will we ever learn?

It wasn't long before Casey asked his dad to help him buy a motorcycle. That was early in 1986.

"I promise, Dad, I'll take care of it, and with the money I'm making, I can pay for it easier than a car."

Ted sat down in his lounge chair, and flipped on the TV like he hoped the situation would go away. But it didn't. Casey persisted. He was good at being sincere and penitent.

Needless to say, in several weeks Casey ended up with a 1986 Yamaha Endura. To our surprise, he kept up the payments. However, the neighborhoods he lived in were hazardous to the cycle, and he was forever replacing parts and tires.

Telephone calls from Casey were frequent, he was good about that. One day, though, his call and astonishing news took me completely by surprise.

* * *

SUB CHAPTER TWO

After my parents moved to California, I started a new kind of life. When my sister was out at night, Mom or Dad would call to see if I was home by nine o'clock. I didn't care whether I was or not. What could they do to me from fifteen hundred miles away? I was having the time of my life. My new business was stripping down cars. My buddies and I stored tires, stereos, wheels and everything we stripped in the basement of Gina's house. She had no idea what I was up to, didn't know what was in her basement.

In June, when school was over, Dad flew out from San Diego to bring me back with him. We drove my old car, and I can remember how long the trip was because I wanted to smoke but couldn't in front of my dad. I'd always been afraid of him; sometimes I think I still am.

I remember how nice it was to see Mom when we got home. I was closer to her than to Dad, not that I was a mamma's boy or anything. She was softer on me than he was, and I wasn't afraid of her.

I'll have to admit that California was beautiful, but I was so lonely it didn't matter. I'd left all my friends behind, kids I'd grown up with, and I held Dad personally responsible for making me move.

About the third or fourth day after coming out here, I drove down to Mission Bay and a guy parked next to me gave me the finger. I remember thinking, "That would never have happened in Oklahoma", and I wanted to go back there in the worst way.

Then I got sick, maybe because I was so depressed, and all I wanted to do was lie around home or go to the beach. Lying in the sun felt good.

Mom and Dad made me get a job and I resented it. I figured I didn't volunteer to come to this earth, so why should I have to pay my own way. That was my parent's job. But they expected me to work so I could learn to be "responsible". I'll admit that having the money was good for extra things, but I was never satisfied. I always had whatever I wanted, but somehow it was never enough. Maybe I wanted the wrong things.

Soon I had a new friend, a prep cook at the restaurant where I worked. He introduced me to cocaine, and to keep his friendship, I became a regular user. After a few weeks he got a new job at a solar company and helped me get one there, too. I couldn't believe it, but everybody there did coke. People, making sixty or seventy thousand a year, would come back where I worked and give me all the coke I wanted. One of the salesmen gave me a bullet—that's a storage container for cocaine. It had a little valve-like switch on the top of it, which, when twisted, gave out a blast of the powder. I found out that my boss was a big coke dealer in North San Diego County.

After I was hooked and had to start buying it on my own my boss said, "There's a lot of copper lying around here that you can steal and sell down at Rose Canyon Scrapping. Give you all the money you want for the coke." Nice man, huh?

By that time I would do anything to get more stuff. It worked for a while, but eventually the president of the company caught me.

He held me in a formal termination meeting for a couple of hours in his plush office. It was awful. It was like jail, being given the third degree.

"Who else in the company is involved?" he repeated over and over.

Telling on somebody else in the drug business is like an instant death warrant, so I wouldn't tell.

Finally, in disgust, he said, "Tell you what I'm going to do. I'm going to keep your last pay check, and I guess I won't press charges against you."

I heaved a big sigh of relief, and got the hell out of there. The company went out of business not long after that so I used them as a reference for my next job at Kapro Computers. I figured there was no way Kapro could check me out.

I made a new friend at Kapro. One night we went to the beach and got real stoned. That's where I met the girl of my dreams. Mom thought I met her at a party. I got her telephone number and called her the next day. I'll never forget it because it was Mother's Day and I chose to be with this girl instead of with Mom. Bad choice. But I was in love with her and didn't care at the time.

Karen was all I could think of for the next year. Everything I did was for her—not for me or my family—but for her. Her sister, Joyce, taught us how to get money for drugs. Boosting and returning was the easiest way to get money. We would go to a shopping mall, steal something, then take it to the refund counter. It was unbelievable. Instant cash! The three of us could make a thousand dollars a day doing this.

Living at home cramped my style, so I moved in with a guy down by the beach and he showed me how to shoot coke in my veins. I didn't know what a needle felt like and, man, was I scared.

He wrapped the belt around my arm, "Make a fist," he said.

I closed my eyes and felt the needle go in. Then I opened my eyes and saw the coke go in my vein. He removed the belt and the next feeling was the beginning of a new relationship. A gush of air came through my nose, and the taste of coke was in my mouth. My ears

*started to ring, and I was off to the races. It was overwhelming. I used
to say I could see God and his whole family, plus his dog. It's funny
how something so damn unforgiving and deadly can feel so good.*

*After that I was doing everything: cocaine, heroin, acid, pot,
mushrooms, and Karen wasn't important anymore, only the
drugs. I had a motorcycle then and lived in Carlsbad with a
black Mormon. I don't know why I said black because that is
irrelevant. Anyway, I would ride down to a place in Solana Beach
where I could get anything I wanted. People stood around on the
street selling coke and chiva (that's what we called heroin). I
never enjoyed heroin because I preferred going up instead of down.
Some days the needle was in my arm at least forty or forty-five
times. The bruises on my arms were so hard to hide that even on
hot summer days I had to wear long sleeves to hide the bruises.*

*Sometimes when I'd had too much, I thought I would die.
One time after Karen and I had been "up" for several days,
suddenly I couldn't breathe. My chest ached. I laid down to die,
I thought. Karen didn't know what to do. She just paced around
the room, wringing her hands, and watching me. She said she
was afraid if anyone came to help me, they would see the tracks
on her arms and she would be in trouble, too. So she didn't do
anything, but stay with me.*

*I came out of it slowly, hours later, and couldn't believe I'd
lived through it. Fifteen minutes later I was on my feet and had
the needle in my arm again.*

*One night, I was out driving around with a buddy of mine.
We were drinking and a cop pulled us over. "Step out of the car."
he said, then he saw an open] bottle in the car. Well, it's obvious
what happened next. We were hauled off to Vista jail, and my
one phone call went home. Thank God Mom answered and I told
her what happened. She turned away from the phone to talk to
Dad. He exploded.*

"He can just stay there, for all I care," he yelled.

*"We can't do that. I've heard what happens to nice looking
guys in jail," I heard Mom say. She sounded desperate.*

"Well, I'm not going to bail him out,"Dad said.

"I'll go pay the bail if you'll give me the money,"Gina said.

"Give her the money, Ted. We have the cash from the garage sale today." Mom put the phone back to her ear and asked me, "How much is the bail, Casey?"

"$125."

"Good grief, Casey," she said like scolding me. Then she told Gina how much, and I heard Dad grumble as he counted out the money and hand it to Gina.

It was about an hour before I was bailed out. Gina was real sweet about it, although I could tell she was disappointed in me. The really bad times were when I didn't have the money to buy any drugs and went through withdrawal. After a year of this up and down existence, I couldn't stand it anymore.

I knew I had to get away from drugs and all the bad stuff I'd been through. So I did the only thing that could be done. I left Karen, my friends, and family behind to start another new life.

* * *

Chapter Three

A NEW LIFE

CASEY'S voice jumped through the telephone. "Hey, Mom, you'll never guess where I am . . . recruiting station in Oceanside . . . joined the army . . . signed up for four years."

My glass of cranberry juice spilled as I put it down on the glass top kitchen table. "Joined the army?" I stammered. "Why . . . where did this idea come from?" I mopped up the juice with a paper towel, and sat down in a black wicker chair at the table.

"You know what my life has been like, Mom. Big mess, nothing going right. Decided to do something about it. Gotta turn myself around somehow—get away from drugs."

"I don't know what to say. I'm stunned." I screamed to myself, be calm, don't let him know how shocked you are.

He laughed, and said "I was actually in the marines for about thirty minutes then decided I didn't want that much battle training, so I tore up the papers, went across the street and joined the army instead. After my four years, I can go to school on the GI Bill and you guys won't have to pay for it."

Another shock. "Go to school? Are you sure this is Casey talking?"

"I know it sounds strange for me, but that's the plan. Guess I'd better hang up. Can I come for dinner? Let me tell Dad and Gina myself. OK?"

"How can I possibly keep this to myself? Well, I'll try. I'm proud of you, honey. Brave thing to do."

I hung up the phone, and knew I had a smile on my face. Hallelujah, I thought. Some mothers might be horrified at this news, but to me it was a great answer. Now he'll be safe, I hope. Safe in the army, that's funny. He'll have to do what he's told—I really grinned when that thought crossed my mind. It will be impossible to argue with a sergeant or put orders off until it suits him. Hooray! Somebody will actually force him to do what he is told.

I decided to cook one of his favorite dinners. I set the dining room table with navy blue place mats, soft blue flowered Haviland china, and placed a bright pink African violet in the center of the table. After all, it was a special occasion.

It was a brisk autumn day. A cool ocean breeze stirred the coral and palm trees in the back yard and warm sunlight streamed across the living room carpet. All's right with the world, I thought.

When Casey arrived, he peeked in all the pans on the stove, hugged me and said, "Moo Shu Pork and fried rice? All right!" He dipped a spoon in the sesame-soy sauce and made a happy sound as he licked the spoon. I wondered how long it had been since he'd had a decent meal. He was thin and ragged looking, long straggly hair hung over his stooped shoulders. He'll learn to stand up straight in the army, I thought with satisfaction. Visualizing his army haircut I chuckled out loud.

"What's funny?" he asked.

"Thinking about your new army hairdo."

"You don't like my hair?" he teased, flipping it with his fingers.

I didn't reply, just gave him one of those looks a mother gives her child when she knows he already has the answer.

Dinnertime was light and happy. I felt like a dark cloud had lifted from all of us when Casey shared his news with Ted and Gina.

"Where is basic training?" asked Ted.

"Can you believe it? Right back to Oklahoma, Fort Sill. Don't guess I'll have a chance to get over to Tulsa, though."

"I doubt it," Ted said. "They'll keep you busy until you finish."

"What's next after basic?" Gina asked.

"I signed up for special training in jet fuel systems. I'll get a bonus of $1800 for doing it. Figured it was a good idea. I'll go somewhere else for that though."

"What about your motorcycle?" Ted asked. Cars and all types of transportation were a sore subject with Ted and me. His record of responsibility was a disaster. "Are you going to keep it?"

"Sure, I can ride it when I come home on leave."

"What I meant to ask is if you going to finish paying for it?"

Casey looked annoyed. "Why wouldn't I? I'll be getting paid, you know."

"I'm remembering the black Camaro. That one cost us $9200 by the time we finished paying for it, and we had to take it away from you, if you recall."

"And I was the one that had to drive the thing the next

few years. I really hated driving that car. Kids pulled up beside me at stop lights and stared at me like they wondered what an old grey-haired gal like me was doing with that car." I said with a shudder.

"How about the two cars you wrecked. Boy, Mom and Dad were mad. Remember that?" Gina asked her brother.

"I must have been crazy to buy you the motorcycle in the first place. But, I repeat, what about it? Another thing we have to consider is where to store the thing while you're gone," Ted said glancing over at me.

Casey remained quiet during this review of past mistakes. Not much he could say anyway. It was all sadly true. "Maybe you could ride it, Dad. You'd look good on it," he said, grinning at his father.

Ted chuckled and, surprisingly, said, "I just might do that."

We all laughed at the mental picture of Ted astride Casey's red, white, and blue Honda, helmet and all.

"Seriously, Dad, I'll pick up the payments when my pay starts coming in."

Gina and I glanced at each other with a 'here comes another fight' look, while Ted settled back in his chair. I could see the wary expression in his eyes. But because we all recognized Casey's attempt to change his life there was no argument. It was so easy to believe Casey's intentions. One look into his bright blue eyes and I was always hooked. He promised faithfully this time he'd make his promise good. I stole another look at Ted's eyes. "We'll see," they said.

About a month passed before Casey was scheduled to leave. He didn't say anything about the delay but we suspected that he hadn't passed the tests for drugs and had to wait until he tested clean. Then he called one day and told us he was shipping out the last week in October.

Casey's progress during basic was steady, winning honors and finishing in the top ten of his platoon. We were so proud of him, always knew he had capabilities never tapped.

He came home for Christmas, arrived on December 19 and had to return January 3. Gina was at work when his plane came in, but Karen insisted on coming with us to pick him up at the airport. The change in him was evident right away. He was quieter, strangely reserved, and seemed ill-at-ease while we had lunch out before taking him home. Never did find out why. He was as uncommunicative as ever during his visit. Most of the time he was off on his motorcycle with Karen. We enjoyed his stay, however, and hated to see him leave again.

"When is your graduation?" I asked over the phone several months later. "We want to come."

"Oh, Mom, it'll last about ten minutes. And besides I'll be shipped out right after it's over. You guys don't need to come," he said matter-of-factly, deciding for us.

I don't know why we agreed, maybe because it was a long trip. Looking back we recognize it as a big mistake. We missed an important event in his life. Couldn't figure out why he was so emphatic about our not being there with him, but he was evasive, as usual. Someday I hoped we could learn to talk to each other, really talk, for a change, and *listen* to each other. After completing basic he was transferred to Aberdeen Proving Grounds, Maryland, for six months. We wished we had gone to his graduation when we found out how far away he would be for a while. Phone calls were frequent and happy. He was enjoying himself, studying hard, and making good grades. Then an unexpected thing happened.

Karen flew to Maryland the day before he finished his training. Casey called to tell us they planned to be married in two days. We wanted to be there, so did Karen's

parents, but Casey said, "We just want to do this on our own."
Again, no explanation, just a flat "no" to all of us.

"What's the matter—didn't you know we'd object?
We've missed everything else important in your life lately,
I guess it's only fitting to miss your wedding, too." I was
furious and didn't try to hide it. I'd hoped his affair with
Karen would end when he went away. Now he would be
married to her. That's what I was angry about more than
anything. A bad alliance if there ever was one.

"Well, I know you and Dad don't like her, but—"

"Don't start giving me a guilt trip, Casey. I'm sure we'll
be able to handle it OK." In a half-hearted attempt to make
peace I said, "I do wish you well, you know that, and want
you to be happy." Why do parents always say that I wondered?
Silence hung between us like gray fog. "Are
you being transferred right away?" I managed to say.

"Shipping out in four days. Going to Colorado. Gotta
go now. Bye, Mom. I love you. Tell Dad and Gina I love
them, too. I'll call when I get to Fort Carson."

He loves us so much we can't be with him on his wedding
day, I muttered to myself after he hung up. Well, that's
that. One more normal day at home, missing out on another
memorable time in our son's life. Maybe someday
I'll understand all this. One time, just one time in my life
I'd like to rant and rave and really say what's on my mind,
but there I was still holding it all in. Maybe eventually I'll
explode and disappear in a puff of smoke.

I complained to Ted when he came home from work
and he remained quiet and withdrawn. Funny, he's usually
the one who says what he thinks. Always know exactly
where he stands on anything. I should be more like that,
but then what could either of us say at this point. We each
knew how the other felt.

When Gina arrived home from work and found out
about the wedding she laughed, and with a bit of sarcasm

said, "I hope he's happy with her, but I'll bet she brings him nothing but grief."

I realized then that Gina probably knew Karen better than any of us. And as it turned out, her remark about Karen was prophetic.

* * *

SUB CHAPTER THREE

It was October 29, 1986 when I left home for basic training. A cold wind was pushing inland off the drab Pacific that day. I stayed at a hotel that night down in San Diego. The next morning a group of us flew to Fort Sill, Oklahoma. A bus took all of us to the receiving station where we stayed for three days. All the guys there were very nice to us. They kept us busy with paperwork, shots, paperwork, haircuts, clothes, paperwork, and more paperwork. Speaking of hair, I didn't have any left after the butcher got through with me. Bald as a brick. When it was time to go on to our unit we were loaded into a bus. Each of us carried about a hundred-fifty pounds of junk, so it was hard to move very fast. We were crowded in like cattle—which is why it is called a cattle truck. Nobody said anything and it was pretty dark in there. After my eyes got used to the dark I looked around, and there he was—a man . . . a man with a round hat on his head, with no emotion in his face, looking at no one. This was the beginning of the hell I had heard about.

Without warning the truck stopped. The guy next to me said, "Shit, here we go."

Three doors slammed open and there they were—ten more of those sons of bitches in round hats. Then the screaming started. "Out. Out of the fucking truck."

The army is definitely not the place for a religious person. If you are not cussing when you go in you can bet you will by the time you get out. Of course, I'm no angel in the cussing department myself, and those s.o.b.'s let us have it all.

"Out! Out! Move," those round hats screamed. "Pick up this piece of shit."

We stumbled all over each other, and the drill sergeants threw stuff around us. Some miracle found me running up a single flight of stairs to what would be my home for the next twelve weeks. It was a large bay room. Fifty bunks lined up in four rows. It looked like a prison. Everything was white and plain.

After running back downstairs to get our linens we assembled upstairs again to inventory our gear.

"What are you looking at?" one of the drill sergeants screamed at a guy down the way. "Do you like me? Do you think I'm cute? You must be a fag. And if you are a fag just get the hell out right now because if I catch you looking at my ass I'll kill you."

The kid started to cry. I couldn't believe it. And here we were, trapped. What made me think I wanted to do this anyway? Too late now.

One thing I'd always had trouble with was listening to authority figures and this was the wrong place to be with a problem like that.

At night, lying in my bunk, I thought about how happy I was about going to the army, when I enlisted, that is. It was a new start and everything. But that day I boarded the bus in Oceanside to go down to San Diego I wasn't so sure. All the fear inside took over. I cried like a baby and hadn't even left town yet. I was so scared. Maybe somewhere deep down inside I knew I was on my way to hell—as if I hadn't already been there.

It was hard knowing I was an addict and didn't get along with my family because of it but, one thing for sure, all through my childhood they had loved me no matter what I did. A lot of kids can't say that.

Basic training consisted of many things: marksmanship, grenades, physical training, and the most important was discipline.

I made expert in marksmanship and grenades. I was good at throwing things. I'd been pitcher in little league baseball in school. Discipline came hard.

Physical training started off slow for me, I was in such bad shape from all the drugs, but I got stronger as I went along. Every muscle in my body ached all the time. Every time we made a mistake of any kind the drill sergeant said, "Drop!" Then we had to do 20 push-ups and say, "Thank you, drill sergeant, for conditioning my mind, body, and soul. Feel free to do so at any time." Incredible.

After basic I was awarded a letter of commendation for being the distinguished honor grad of my graduating class. Mom and Dad got a letter from the CO about it and I think they were proud of me for a change.

When it was all over I was sad, believe it or not. I made real friends there. We went in boys and came out men with a bond holding us together. I hated to say goodbye but had to move on to AIT, special training.

I had chosen fuel and electrical repair for special schooling and was sent to Aberdeen Proving Grounds, Maryland. It was a beautiful place and I kept busy with school. After a while, though, we had more freedom—freedom to go to bars and get drunk. And there were plenty of women. It seemed like heaven. Somehow they were easy to get and I had my share. In the six months I was there, I ended up sleeping with sixteen women.

We called it "The Game". We'd go to a bar and pick out the nicest looking woman there, which wasn't hard because there were a lot of ugly ones around, let me tell you. The guy that got the prettiest woman won the game. Another guy named Butler and I won the most. We were looked up to because of this talent.

Something was missing, though. The drugs. In the back of my mind I knew they would be coming soon.

One night a bunch of us guys went into a crumby little bar looking for girls. I sat next to a hooker at the bar. She wasn't as young as most of the ones I'd seen, looked like she'd done a lot of living. We talked a few minutes, don't remember what about. Then for some odd reason I asked her, "Can you get some coke?"

"Sure, baby, I can get you anything you want. You ready now?"

"Sure," I said, wide eyed.

"Hang on a bit, I'll be back." She left to get the coke and when she came back she said, pressing up close to me, "You know, I probably do this a different way than you do."

"What do you mean?"

"I shoot it."

"So do I," I said, and off we went to the bathroom.

She used the needle first then handed it to me with her blood still in it. I didn't think about it at the time but later I worried about AIDS.

So there I was. Drugs and alcohol back in my life, right back where I started from.

Karen came to Maryland to see me and we decided to get married. One night we went to a hotel with another couple and while Karen and my buddy went to the store, my buddy's girl friend said, "You know what I really want to do?"

"No. What?"

"I really want to kiss you."

I knew then I didn't want to get married yet. Too much fooling around to do. So the next morning I told Karen, "Let's wait a while."

"Wait a while," she screamed. "Why do you think I came all the way across country? What'd you ask me for if you don't want to."

"Karen . . ."

"Go to hell. I'm goin' home. Let me know when you're ready."

Seemed like all we ever did was fight.

Several months later, just before graduation from AIT, she returned and again we decided to get married. I'd found out I could get eight hundred dollars more pay if I got married, so I said, "What the hell. Let's do it."

The night before our wedding we were in a bar, of all places. After a while, Karen finished a drink, rubbed her eyes and said, "I've got a headache. Goin' to my room. See ya later."

Next thing I knew, I began hitting on a girl sitting next to me. We ended up in the room next to Karen's. I was afraid Karen would find out but she never said anything about it. The next day we were married. I got drunk and passed out by two o'clock that afternoon. Obviously a marriage headed for disaster.

The next day I graduated AIT, Karen went back home until I could send for her, and I was transferred to Fort Carson, Colorado.

* * *

Chapter Four

EASY MONEY

CASEY and Karen found an apartment in Colorado Springs not far from the base and settled down. Karen worked from time to time but never could hold a job very long. There was always some valid reason like back trouble or illness. It would have been nice for her to help out with the expenses because Casey's pay wasn't very much, but he said they were doing all right. Somehow they managed to buy a used truck so Casey could get to and from the base.

Casey's reports about his work on the base were favorable. He was assigned to the supply room and after a short time was given some computer training. All the supply records were then put into the computer and he was in charge. Everything sounded good, and he seemed upbeat and interested in what he was doing.

They came home for Christmas that year and stayed with us most of the time. Once again we noticed their restlessness. They seemed happy except for an incident one night during dinner. The five of us had settled down at the dinner table when Karen suddenly got up and went outside.

"What's wrong?" I asked Casey.

"I don't know, Mom. Maybe she wanted a smoke."

I couldn't tell whether he was annoyed with me for asking or at Karen for leaving without a word.

"Isn't that a bit strange after we just sat down to dinner?" Ted asked.

"I'll go see about her," our son said, throwing his napkin down on the table.

The rest of us glanced at each other in wonder and kept on eating. We could hear raised voices but couldn't understand the words. Finally they both came back inside and sat down at the table.

Karen tried to eat, but got up quickly again and rushed outside.

"What's going on," Ted said angrily. Enough was enough for him.

"She wants to go down to the beach and see a friend. I guess I'll go with her," Casey explained. He jumped up and walked out leaving us with blank expressions.

Later we learned she wanted to go and buy some drugs. It was a preamble to things to come.

In January 1988 Gina graduated from National University with an accounting degree. To celebrate we took her to Hawaii and had a glorious time. Something about Hawaii made me think all was right with the world.

After we returned she became engaged to Zack, a fellow she had met when she bought her Hyundai. The wedding was planned for early summer, however, as time passed Gina had doubts about him. Finally he confessed to her that he was a drug addict and needed time to work things out. Serious flaws in his character came to light soon after that. Gina was heart sick about the break up but this resolved into gratitude that they had not married. She was well rid of him and knew it. Another close encounter with drug addiction.

One morning after Ted left for his office, I was cleaning up the breakfast dishes and the telephone rang.

"Hi, Mom," Karen said in her soft little voice. I felt trouble through the wire. "What's going on?" I asked, gazing through the kitchen window at the early morning haze.

"We need some help. I wrote some checks and we're overdrawn. If they're returned to the stores it'll be reported on Casey's record at the base and he'll get in a whole lot of trouble."

I could really feel the bite now. Even so, I plunged right on to the inevitable request. "What's on your mind, Karen?"

"We need $75 to cover what I've written and need it today. If you send it by Western Union we'll have it in plenty of time."

"I've never sent money that way. What do I do?" I asked, fool that I am.

She explained what to do in great detail. I knew then she'd had plenty of practice with this method of obtaining quick funds.

She had me where it hurts . . . doing anything to protect my son. I agreed, hung up the phone, grabbed my purse, and hurried to the Western Union office in the shopping center not far from home. I wondered how Karen knew where it was since she had not lived in Encinitas but in Solana Beach, a few miles south of us.

On the way, I decided not to tell Ted about it. No need to worry him. It's only $75, I reasoned. This was just another little secret anyway. I could write a check from my own account I had set up from my advertising sales. Someday I'd probably have to stop these deceptions, but I told myself it was for Ted's own good.

Time passed and, foolish me, I expected a note of

thanks, or at least a note saying everything was all right. This didn't happen and several weeks later Karen called again.

"The truck's out of whack and it'll cost $150 to fix it. Casey has to have it to get to the base every morning so we have to get it fixed. Could you send the money by Western Union right away?"

"You need it today? Couldn't you have given me a little time to mail it? It costs quite a bit to send it that way, you know."

"I'm sorry, Mom. But we do need it today."

Every time she called me Mom I felt a little twinge go through me. And a little nagging feeling of distrust began growing inside me. But I shoved it aside, since I am by nature a trusting person, in this case a fool. It was strange, I thought, that their money situation had suddenly become so acute. They'd never asked for money before. Needless to say, I sent the money to them, without any more questions, and didn't tell Ted about it.

Gina came over for dinner the next week and while we were cleaning up the kitchen, she said with disgust, "Guess what? Karen called me yesterday and wanted $150."

I almost dropped a plate and glanced around to make certain Ted couldn't hear. "I sent them the same amount last week. You didn't send it, did you?"

"Sure. She sounded so desperate."

"Don't tell me you sent it by Western Union?"

"She said they had to have it quick."

"What was the money for this time?"

"I hate to tell you, Mom, but she said Casey was in jail and the money was for bail."

"In jail? What for?"

"DWI."

The silence between us was sad and heavy like all the old troubles were hanging in the air. The army was supposed to be his salvation from the old ways, yet here they were again.

Gina interrupted my thoughts. "But, I don't think he was in jail at all. I think the money was for drugs and they lied to get it."

"For drugs? I thought he was over that since he'd been in the army. Stupid. Mothers are so stupid. We put ourselves in this dream world that everything is rosy and all we're doing is fooling ourselves. We should be able to see through all the junk."

"I'm not sure about the drugs. That's just what I think," she said trying to comfort me.

But I believed her because she knew him pretty well and understood his problems far better than Ted and I.

The next week my brother, Paul, called me from Palo Alto with more distressing news. "I had a call from Karen today," he said. "Their truck broke down and needs repairs to the tune of $350."

"Oh, no, Paul. You didn't send it, did you?"

"At first I said no, but after thinking it over I said I'd send it to them and it would be their Christmas present and they wouldn't need to pay it back. I don't know why I called you about it." He chuckled as if apologizing for telling me. Then he added, "And I didn't send it by Western Union either, which they begged me to do. I told them if they wanted it bad enough they'd have to wait for the regular mail."

Why wasn't I that smart, I thought. Then I told him the long sad tale of what had been going on with them.

"I should have called you first, I guess, but it's too late now. What's done is done," he said.

Questions nagged at me. Why were all the telephone calls from Karen? Why didn't Casey call? After all, the calls were to his own family. Or had they called her family as well? And why was money so urgently needed?

I'd like to say that Casey called and explained on his

own, but he didn't. Gina took matters into her own hands
this time.

* * *

SUB CHAPTER FOUR

*I was especially good at talking Karen into doing anything. I told
her to call for the money and she did it. We'd run out of places to
go for cash, already sold a lot of stuff and had no where else to
turn.*

*Conning Mom and Dad and the rest of the family was a
terrible thing to do, but addicts don't care what we do or who we
con as long as we get our next fix.*

*Even though I made some bad mistakes and screwed myself
up with the army, my job was still important to me and I couldn't
afford to get caught shoplifting. Guess I must not have cared if
Karen got caught.*

*It was like I was two people. One guy had to get up each
morning and do PT, running, pushups, and situps. Somewhere
deep inside me the values and morals my folks bred into me were
still there fighting with the other guy who was a drunk and a
druggie. It was hard work keeping up that kind of pace. It would
have been easier being just a druggie without all the other stuff
running around in my head. But I did it for a long time and did
it very well, thank you very much.*

* * *

Chapter Five

A HELL OF A WOMAN

DEAR Casey,

I'm writing you because I don't believe you were in jail the other night when Karen called. I think you wanted the money for drugs. I want you to know that I love you very much, but I think it's time for you to quit lying to yourself and your family. You should tell Mom and Dad about your drug problem because they are here to help you as always.

The decision is yours to make. I can't make you change. Mom and Dad can't make you change. You have to decide to do it yourself. But don't expect us to trust you for a while.

You've pretty well broken the trust between us and will have to prove yourself to

us. The thing is, you have to be honest for
once in your life and then maybe you can work
out your problems.

Remember, I love you and I'm here for
you just like I always have been.

Love, Gina

Casey phoned a few days after he received the letter.
Somehow it seemed Casey and I lived our entire
relationship over the telephone. "Hi, Mom," he said in a
low voice that usually meant trouble.

"What's wrong, honey?" Might as well ask and not waste
time, I thought. Collect calls can get pretty expensive.

"I have something to tell you, Mom. You won't like it,
but it has to be said."

He was right—I didn't like what he had to say. And I
wished Ted were home so I wouldn't have to repeat it all
later. No more lying to Ted, no more evasions. For once in
my life, I would have to lay it all out for him. We could deal
with it together.

Casey's words came in a low monotone, devoid of
feeling. I sat at the kitchen table and listened.

"I guess you've known about me and the drugs. Been
into that for a long time since I was a kid. Since Karen and
I've been here it's gotten worse. We've shoplifted and written bad checks for drug money. I got a DWI and was arrested once and overdosed once, too. We've borrowed
money against my pay and the army is threatening discharge
if I don't straighten myself out. Oh, yeah, and Karen's pregnant, about three months along."

Karen pregnant? Hard to be glad about that.

Well, he had laid it on the line, the whole sordid mess.
But I had to ask, "Is that all? Have you told me everything?"

He was quiet a minute, then said, "All the money we
asked you for lately was for drugs. The reasons were lies."

"One thing I'd really like to know—why did Karen make all the calls?"

"I just couldn't do it, too chicken."

"Good grief, Casey, what can I say. I know it was hard for you to admit all this." I paused a minute then said, "I'll have to tell your dad. I'm not keeping any more secrets from him. It's not fair. And hasn't done you any good either."

"I know."

"What will you do next?"

"Appeal the discharge. I'd like to stay in the army and finish what I started for once. Right now they're not letting me work and I have too much time on my hands. The doc says I have to have my gall bladder out soon. Been sick a lot. I'm going in for a blood test tomorrow."

"Your gall bladder . . . is the operation dangerous? Have you been having trouble very long?"

"Not long, Mom, and it'll be OK."

"Call the minute you know more about it, will you?" Not surprising that he'd been sick after abusing his body so much. The thought of someone cutting on my son made me feel sick. What else could happen, I wondered.

Tears poured down Gina's cheeks when we discussed the effect her letter had on Casey. "I poured out my heart for God to help me write that letter . . . to say the right things. And the neat thing was that Casey said he was praying too, for help from somewhere. And the letter changed everything . . . for all of us."

Knowing that my children were each praying for answers brought us all together in my thought. We had hope.

He wasn't able to get a Christmas leave that year. Needless to say it was a different kind of holiday. Part of our family was missing and in trouble. After Gina told us about the letter she had written her brother we understood why he finally confessed.

Several days after Christmas a letter from him arrived.

"Dear Mom and Dad,

It's Christmas Eve and I'm feeling kind of sad and low. I haven't been doing drugs but everything I've done lives inside me. The hardest part of it all is lying to everyone, especially my own family. Now I pray and hope you will not disown me. I need to know how you feel about me right now.

Thank you for the gifts. The sweat suit really comes in handy when I play racquet ball. I'm pretty good, too! Those chocolate mints really make me remember the past when I'd find them in my stocking every Christmas morning.

I know I let you down and let myself down, too. But I'll make it. Mom, you say success follows failure and I'm really going to live up to that.

I had an interesting experience. The Army Criminal Intelligence Division asked me to talk to some students about drugs at a high school. So I did. There were five hundred students there. Afterwards the principal told me she knew that I had helped at least one student that she knew.

She hugged me, said, "Thank you, son, and good luck." I felt like I had done some good for others and I felt important.

I love you both very much and I'm sorry for what's happened. But thank God for my sister who wrote such a strong letter. She's a hell of a woman.

Love always,
Casey

* * *

SUB CHAPTER FIVE

It was strange that all throughout my using, I prayed to God to help me survive all the crap but I never thought for one minute He was actually listening. That anybody cared or would listen never crossed my mind.

I was at the bottom of the barrel. My first sergeant refused to help me and left me without any hope of surviving. My last few months in the army were the worst. I was shooting up on anything I could get and drinking like crazy. In a way I think I wanted to get high, close my eyes, and never come back to this horrible place called earth.

There is no truth or honesty on that side of the world, people are cold and look down on anyone living that way. Everyone around me knew I was a loser and treated me like one. Maybe that's how African Americans have felt for years because of the treatment they get from the white man.

One morning after a sleepless night I heard mail call out in the hall. Somebody knocked on my door and handed me my mail. Most all the mail I got those days were bills, six or seven at least. But in this stupid stack of bills was a letter from Gina.

I sat down on my bunk and opened it very slowly, afraid of what it would say. But it was a letter of hope. She was there if I needed her. After all the rejections in my life, there in her words, even though she let me know I was wrong, I found hope. She cared and let me know it.

I always knew my parents cared what was happening to me, but I was afraid of their reaction if they actually heard the truth. Dad was strict and a powerful man. Oh, yeah, stubborn as hell, too. What's funny is that I'm just like him so we've had some big disagreements.

With the letter, though, I had a way out. What Gina said was the answer and the only way to follow. It saved my life.

The door was finally open to the little cell I had built around me. It was a solitary confinement cell with no light coming in. Now the door was open. The light was so damn bright it left no doubt in my mind. The hiding was over.

* * *

Chapter Six

DEAD ENDS

WEEKS stretched into months. Casey called us often to keep us informed about his status with the discharge and his health. After the gall bladder surgery in January 1989 the doctor ordered inactive duty and the idleness was hard for him to take. Putting a drug addict in that situation on a drug infested base was risky.

His mood was solemn and despondent. Yet, for once in his life, he wanted to tell us everything, not holding back. Sometimes we found out more than we wanted to know. Since long distance calls were expensive, I suggested sending him a tape recorder so he could tape what he wanted to say without time limits. Once in a while he called simply to hear friendly voices.

One day two tapes arrived and I settled down on the sofa to listen. I was totally unprepared for what he had to say. His voice was low and halting at first, but as the words poured out he became more at ease. I closed my eyes and listened:

"Well, here goes. I hope I can do this OK. I guess I'll start back when Karen and I came to this base. We kept on with the drugs and by October 1988 we were doing up to $800 a day in crack. We sold some of our things to get the money, shoplifted, wrote bad checks, and owed everybody we knew, including the army. Then I was picked up on a DWI and given an Article 15. That's a punishment statement for bad conduct.

To make matters worse the gall bladder trouble brought on more complications. My blood tests were positive for drugs and the surgery was put off until I could test clean. I managed to stay off the stuff and finally tested clean for the operation.

When they opened me up my left lung collapsed, so they stopped right there, and rescheduled the surgery. When I woke up the doc asked, "How many cigarettes do you smoke a day?"

"About four packs," I told him. Man, I thought I was dying. I stayed clean for another week and didn't smoke as much then went in again for the operation.

Lying there in the hospital I knew it was time to get some help. Karen was there when I was released and on the way home we decided to go and see my first sergeant to ask for his help. His name was Walzack, not an easy guy to know, but I had to go to him first. Channels you understand.

His office looked like the president's office, eagles and flags everywhere. The glare from the wide windows was almost blinding and we had to sit facing it. One wall displayed an Article 15 chart. Putting it up on the wall like that looked to me like he was bragging about all the guys in trouble. You can bet my name was up there with the rest.

"Top," I said, not wasting any time, "we've got a drug problem and need help."

He glanced up at the chart on the wall beside him, shook his little shaved head, and said, "Look, Harper, I know the trouble you're in. You're asking too late."

I stood up feeling like I was going to cry, I was that desperate. After all those years on drugs I was finally asking for help and this creep was refusing. "Sir, I need help. My wife needs help. I'll probably be dead in thirty days without some help." I shot a quick look at Karen. She was just sitting there with her head down. I wondered why she didn't say anything to back me up. "Come on, Top," I said, turning back to face the sergeant. "Do something for us, anything."

"You could try to stay off the stuff for a couple weeks. If you can do that I'll see about getting you a counselor." He was shuffling papers around on his desk and spoke with the emotion of a man ordering pizza. What a jerk.

After we got home that day I called a drug rehab center in the mountains nearby. They said twenty-one days was all I needed for a session and I had thirty-two days leave accrued. I was excited about it and called Walzack.

"No, Harper, I told you it's too late. I'm not letting you go."

He slammed down the phone leaving me with nothing. It's not fair, I thought. Then I got mad at myself for getting in this mess. Hell, I joined the army to get straight, serve my four years, then go to school. I sure loused it up.

The next few weeks I tried to stay clean—didn't do too good either. Then Walzack called and told me to get myself over to the counselor's office. The jerk did come through, after all.

I don't remember the counselor's name, but she was an odd little person. She had stringy hair, wore no make-up, was kind of bland looking—antiseptic and unfeeling. Some counselor. Beethoven played in the background. I recognized it from the music you play, Mom. I was there an hour every week and it turned out to be no big deal. Look, I didn't want sympathy, or somebody looking down her nose at me. I wanted guidelines, anything constructive. But all she did was threaten.

Everything she said was based on fear, pure raw fear. "Take the test again," she said. "If it comes out hot then we'll wait another thirty days and take another. And if that comes out hot, too, then we'll just kick you out of this army." She might as well have added, "Ho, hum."

She was no help at all. Fear tactics don't work because addicts are afraid all the time anyway, afraid of life itself— afraid going to buy the stuff, going to the middle of no-where with guns all around. But, hell, fear is overcome real easy. Just take a hit and fear goes away."

At this point, I cut off the tape. His troubled voice was like agony to me. I stared outside into the bright sunshine, bathing my garden with warmth. Tiny gray birds splashed in the birdbath, and a gentle breeze stirred the coral tree. I thought, what a sane world I live in. Will my son ever know a world like this?

I went to the kitchen, brewed a cup of tea, and went back to my place on the sofa. When a sense of calm returned, I switched on the tape and sank back into Casey's pain:

"The Article 15 came back to haunt me. It was read at the battalion level by a lieutenant colonel. He said, "This dishonorable discharge of yours could be turned around. We would be willing to upgrade it to general discharge with some help from you. The CID needs some help from the inside with drug busts."

"The CID? What . . . ?"

"Criminal Investigation Division," he answered.

"I don't know about that, Sir. My wife might be in danger. I can't risk it." I wanted to sit down but he had me at attention.

Obviously that's not what he wanted to hear because he fastened his cold dark eyes on mine and never blinked. "Harper, why don't you tell me how you handle so much cocaine without dealing to the other soldiers in the company?"

It was an accusation, not a question. Hell, he thought I was dealing, and besides, how did he know how much stuff I got. "I never sold in my life, Sir, because once it comes into my apartment it never leaves. My wife and I do it all," I told him.

He jumped up, picked up an ax handle from his desk, leaned across the desk into me, and shook the ax handle in my face. "Harper, I'd like to take you down range and beat the living crap out of you." His face turned deep red, and his voice was low and pinched.

This guy was about fifty years old, a little over five-feet tall, with a macho image that he's better than anybody. I could have punched him out right there and felt good about it, but, hell, I knew better. I was already in enough trouble. I said nothing and took the Article 15 punishment like a good little soldier. I had to wonder why he had that ax handle on his desk and how many other guys he'd threatened with it.

My punishment was called Non-Judicial For Wrongful Use Of Cocaine. It meant a fine of $300 a month for two months, and forty-five days of extra duty. I was demoted from an E4 Specialist to a private, which meant a cut in pay. I filed an appeal but the colonel turned it down.

We were at rock bottom by then, no way to live on half pay. We sold everything we had and that's when I sent Karen home to live with her parents. She was four months pregnant. I hoped she would stay clean until after the baby came, but she didn't. She just kept right on doing the drugs.

I had my pay checks forwarded to her so the army wouldn't take out what I owed them. But that was a bad idea since she spent most of it on crack and stuff. And I had no idea what else lay ahead of me."

"Karen," I muttered in disgust, turning off the tape machine. Every time I thought about her I got angry. It was easy to heap blame on her, although I knew Casey was as much to blame as she was. But she was a part of our family, and like it or not, was carrying my grandchild. Wouldn't it be a blessing if the baby could pull us all together? I thought about the times I'd spent with Karen since she had been back home with her parents. We had lunch together and talked many times. Her interests were few and conversations were difficult, but we became friends, I thought, and my thoughts about her began to change. Her childlike ways tugged at my heart.

I don't recall what we said to each other during our visits. I do remember her wounded eyes, the way her lips quivered and turned down at the corners. I saw how vulnerable she was and wanted to help her. But it never happened.

She was extremely thin, still smoking and doing drugs and didn't look pregnant at all. One time I asked her, "Aren't you afraid you'll harm the baby if you don't stop?"

She just shrugged her shoulders and looked away. I have since learned that addicts don't care about anything but their next fix. A few months later she said she had quit, but I discovered she was a very good liar. Addicts do that, too, and very well, I found out.

I recall an episode when some friends from Tulsa were visiting us. We were playing cards and enjoying ourselves when Karen suddenly appeared at our door. Acting strange was not unusual for her, but that time her behavior was really off the wall.

We introduced her to our friends, then she asked to use the rest room. I noticed Ted watching her after she came out of the bathroom. In a few minutes she came back in the living room and said, "Can I go in the guest room and change my clothes?" She had a shirt and some jeans in her hand.

She turned and walked toward the other room.

Before I could answer, Ted jumped up and said, "No, wait a minute." He rushed into the guest room.

"But I just want to change," Karen said impatiently.

"Just wait a minute," I told her, wondering what was going on.

Soon Ted came back and said, "OK, you can go in there now."

After she left the room, he whispered to our friend, "Bob, your money clip was laying on top of the TV and I knew she must have seen it when she went in there a minute ago. So I went in and put it in my pocket. I think she would have taken it. Else why was she so insistent on going in there? She could have changed clothes in the bathroom."

Needless to say we were all shocked.

Later when I told Gina about it, she told me she believed Karen stole her pearl necklace some time before that. Gina was sentimental about the necklace because my brother had given it to her when she was a baby. It was called an "Add-A-Pearl" necklace, adding a pearl each birthday. So from then on we were suspicious when she wandered around our home and kept a wary eye on her.

I don't know how long I'd been sitting there lost in my thoughts. One more tape to play. Better get on with it.

* * *

Chapter Seven

GUNS AND WIRES

MY cup of tea was ice cold and I decided not to bother pouring another cup, probably forget to drink it, too. I removed the first tape from the player and inserted the second one. This time I didn't sit down but paced around the living room while Casey's solemn voice spoke to me ;

"After Karen left for California I moved into the barracks hoping I could file an appeal against the discharge and stay in the army. When I got to the barracks I asked Walzack what room I was in.

"Room 118," he said grinning at me.

"But that's a transit room, Sir."

"That's right, soldier. We're moving you out of the army."

Discharged, already? I couldn't answer. Nice way to find out.

Later that day First Sergeant Brubaker came into my room. Brubaker, what a name. It fit him. Stern guy, stony cold face. I snapped to attention. He pointed his finger at me and said, "I just wanted you to know where you stand. You can get out of the army one way, or you can get out the hard way. If you want to make it the hard way and cause me a bunch of hassles, I'll plant a bag of marijuana on you and send you off to Leavenworth. You got that?"

I got it all right and figured that was it for me. It was clear no appeal was to be filed if Brubaker had anything to do with it. Funny thing though. I still wanted to stay in the army.

The CO and the lieutenant colonel recommended an honorable discharge under general conditions, but the big shot colonel said no, it would be dishonorable. I was going out in disgrace and he was making sure of it.

Then something unusual happened. The CID called me into their all white, no windows office. They made the same offer the lieutenant colonel had made, to make drug busts for an upgrade on my discharge. After thinking about it a few minutes I said, "You might have to relocate me so I won't get killed after it's over." One of the guys said, "Well, the only way we'd do that is if you're threatened and the threat is verified."

I said, "Forget it. Those guys don't threaten. They just shoot you." While I was shaking my head saying no to them they kept talking, putting on the pressure.

I was over a barrel and they knew it. I was scared, but finally agreed. "Who is it I'm supposed to bust? Do I know them?" I sat down and felt like I was crawling into a black hole.

"Only one man this first time, and yes, you know him all right. It's your roommate."

My roommate? The room went dark. Man, did I feel trapped. But I had to do it. No choice.

I spent days there going over procedure and training with all the recording equipment and signals that were to be used. It was weird, I had gone from one extreme into another world. Why in hell couldn't I find a happy medium somewhere?

They gave me a hundred dollars to give to Fred, my roommate, so he could get me the coke, but when drugs are involved something always seems to go wrong. He gave the money to a friend to make the buy but the friend never came back. The whole time we were under surveillance and I was wired with a voice activator and microphone, so the CID knew I hadn't screwed up. The thought crossed my mind that they were testing me at first with a small amount of cash. After a few more failed attempts everything seemed to quiet down. I was getting anxious for something to happen.

A couple of nights later, Richard, a big black guy, saw me downstairs in the barracks and pulled me over into a corner where no one would hear, and said, "We got some crack upstairs. Come on up. We'll party after we take care of some business."

Panic hit me in the gut and my mouth went numb. "Sure, I said, trying to act cool. "I'll be right there." I'd have to wing it on my own with no activator or mike on me.

I called my CID connection and told her, "It's going down in room 210. Better hurry."

"Hang loose," she said. "We're on the way."

Climbing the stairs was like being in a tunnel with no light at either end. But I hurried so the guys wouldn't be suspicious.

Everything is concrete in the barracks—walls, floors, ceilings—all white, cold as hell. Since the room was on the third floor I knew a quick escape was impossible.

I reached the room, took a deep shaky breath, and

opened the door. Three guys were in there, already pretty wired. They kept shoving the stuff in my face, it smelled so damn good but I had to stay clean because after every bust a piss test is taken so I had to say no. I gagged, feeling like I was going to throw up.

"Come on, Casey," my roommate said.

"My wife's gonna call in a while. I don't wanta be messed up when she calls," I told them.

"Sure," they said, and kept pushing it at me.

I kept praying for a knock on the door or some sign of the CID. I wasn't too sure about what I was supposed to do when they came. Finally, the knock sounded and I jumped up.

Fred said, "Wait!" but I wasn't about to stop. I was there in a flash. When I opened the door three forty-fives were pointed in my face. I dropped to the floor and put my hands over my head. They could've blown my head off not knowing I was the undercover.

They dragged us out in the hall, slammed us up against a concrete wall, and frisked us. Then one by one, they took us upstairs to the latrine and strip searched us. When nothing was found on me they knew who I was, but I was busted right along with the others to cover me.

Three separate cars took us to the MP station. What a scene that was—people bleeding, drunks everywhere. They stood us about three feet from a wall, facing it, with our hands cuffed behind us. One of the officers barked, "Put your heads on that wall!" We looked at each other and knew there was no way we could get on it. Right quick another officer came up behind and pushed us, one by one— smack, smack, smack, smack—into that wall. My head hurt for a week.

After everyone was processed we were taken back to the barracks. Funny thing, guys arrested like this aren't put in jail right away. They're released on base until after their trial then sent to jail. Bad for me because we were together in the barracks and they were suspicious that I was the snitch. And there was Fred in the bed next to mine. Talk about no sleeping! My lies worked for a while, until one night they got drunk. I tried to stay away from them, but my roommate found me alone lying on my cot. He rushed in, jumped on top of me, and started choking me. I kicked him off and got out of there.

The game room downstairs seemed like a safe place to hide. On Monday morning I called the CID and by three o'clock that afternoon Fred was carted off to jail for good. I never saw him again.

But the CID wasn't through with me yet, not by a long shot. The commander brought me into his windowless pit again, and said, "Harper, you've done a good job for us. That was a hard bust because you just had to be there and go through whatever happened. We want you to help us again and this time we'll be closer at hand for you." He leaned back in his big black chair, stretched himself, and added, "You don't have to do it, of course, but this is someone we really want to get. Maybe you could do it as a favor to me." A sly smile crossed his lips.

Yeah, a favor, I thought. I knew right then I had to do it.

I guess he knew I had agreed because he didn't wait for an answer. He started talking again. "This bust is a woman in your company, an officer. She works both sides of the street, an undercover for us, and a snitch for the dealers on base."

It was easy to see why they wanted to put her away. I asked, "How do I figure in?"

"We know about a shipment coming in soon. We'll let her find out about it, by accident, she'll think, and she'll also find out you're the buyer."

The truth about the whole thing was that she was going to try to bust me while I was busting her. That way the CID would have us both. I knew better than to screw up if I was going to get out of the army. See, she'd been told specifically *not* to buy me any coke, but she did it anyway. The CID knew she would. They were banking on this for the bust.

Several nervous days later she called me and we arranged to meet. I rushed over to the CID office, as I'd been told to do, and told them she'd called me.

They put a voice activator on me. I was wearing my BDU's. They're battle fatigues-six pockets in the pants, four pockets in the shirt, and I had a tee shirt on underneath, so I was bulky enough to hide anything. The voice activator was in the right side pocket of my pants, and the microphone was taped to my chest.

They told me to turn my cap around as a signal to them when the deal went down. Then they handed me the cash for the buy. All that money right there in my hands. I could've taken it and split. Have to keep running the rest of my life, though. Not a good idea. I met the woman, Sheila was her name, as planned and gave her the money. What surprised me was that she already had the coke on her. I put it in my BDU's, and casually turned my hat around, acting cool, I thought. We had a little conversation, but I don't remember what was said. She got into the car and asked me to pull around to the PX. That puzzled me, but I did as she said. She got out, said she'd be right back, and went inside. I wondered where the CID was all this time. Maybe she was calling them to come get me.

An officer came by the car, gave me a sharp stare, and said, "Soldier, you'd better turn that cap around the right way."

I said, "Yes, Sir," but thought, asshole. I did as ordered, but as soon as he disappeared around a corner, I turned the cap around the wrong way again, thinking, where in hell is the CID? I was getting edgy.

Sheila came back, got in the car, and told me to pull around the corner to her barracks. All this going and stopping had me worried. Just as she was getting out of the car three cars roared up behind us. Six guys jumped out, pointed guns at us, and frisked us. They cuffed Sheila and put her in one of the cars. One guy took me over to his car and started removing the voice activator and mike. He said, "OK, Harper, where's the buy?"

Crazy. Here's a cop, already frisked me, knows I have it, yet can't find it on me. I fished the bundle out of a side pocket and gladly handed it over. Later on after Sheila had been taken away, he said, "You should win an Academy Award for your acting. You're good."

I was afraid he had another job in mind. Compliments made me nervous, I guess. But I said, "What do you mean acting? You guys come out here with guns pointed at my head. You scare the shit out of me."

He thought that was funny like I was joking around with him.

The CID came after me one more time before I was finished with them. That bust was a guy who lived in town, off base, and everything went as planned. The thought crossed my mind that maybe I should be a cop when I got out of the army. I'd been living on the edge for a long time anyway."

I heard the tape machine clicking and realized it had turned off. I stared down at my damp hands. Guess I'd been wringing them as I listened. Great relief swept over me, relief that the ordeal was over, at least that part of it was.

* * *

Chapter Eight

SLIPPING THROUGH OUR FINGERS

ONE afternoon in March Karen appeared at my door with a fat letter from Casey. He had asked her to share it with us.

"Come on in. How about a cold drink?" I asked her as I opened the door.

"Gotta get back home. Mom wants to go shopping," she replied, already turning to leave.

"You sure are tiny for a girl expecting this month." I followed her down the front walk.

"Oh, it's in there all right." She laughed and patted her round tummy.

I waved as she drove off, then went back inside, anxious to read Casey's letter.

It was dated March 5, written on the backs of some yellow forms while on extra duty that Sunday night. It read:

Dear Karen,

Well, here I sit thinking how much I'm going to miss

the army even with all the crap lately. I hate to say goodbye to the few friends I have here. But it's you, Gina, Mom, and Dad (my four best friends) who keep me going. You're always there for me when I need you, but, I'm sorry to say, I'm never there if any of you need me. We've been through everything, drugs, going broke, other men, other women, from having everything we wanted to wanting nothing we had. I've never felt so down. "Other than Honorable" that's my title now. Another word for *loser*. My first sergeant told the entire company I was the scum of the company. Two-hundred guys heard him call me that. Everyone laughed. Is this the way I'm going to be looked at the rest of my life? I don't think I can live that way. I don't even know the purpose of my existence. Did God give up on me too? All the time I wonder if I can beat drugs. Are they stronger than me? If so then I don't want to be any longer. I've thought about suicide many times but I know I am loved and always will be loved, no matter what. Nobody can leave all that caring behind. I guess I'm lucky, in a really weird way. It's not right that I give so much pain and get love back. With all this going for me maybe I *can* start over after all.

Are you all right? Is the baby kicking a lot? Soon we'll be a team of three. When you go into labor have your folks call the Red Cross like I told you. Hang in there and I'll be with you soon.

Please show this to my parents. I got a lot out today. Feels good. Proud to be your husband, Love always—

This letter was at once disturbing and comforting and I was grateful that Casey wanted to share it with us. Ted and Gina shared my feelings about it. We each poured over his words many times.

Karen's doctor at Camp Pendleton Marine Base Hospital scheduled weekly visits for her because of her drug addiction. We all knew that the baby would not be released if any signs of addiction were evident after birth. This fear was a constant threat and we prayed for this innocent child's safety. A few weeks before the delivery date the doctor said the fluid surrounding the baby was clear. I didn't know what this meant but surmised it was a good sign since Karen was so happy about it. It seemed logical to assume her condition had improved.

On March 22 Karen went into labor and her family rushed her to the hospital. Lisa, seven pounds, six ounces was born the next day. Karen's mother called us that afternoon to let us know the baby had arrived and mother and daughter were both fine.

I had to wonder why someone in Karen's family didn't call us when she went to the hospital. It would have been nice to know the baby was on the way. Ridiculous, I thought. It was as if we didn't count. They did call the Red Cross as Casey had instructed them to do, but didn't call him.

Casey phoned us the minute he found out and said he had a leave and was hopping a flight the next morning to Edwards Air Force Base, about 150 miles north of us.

My heart pumped with joy as Ted and I watched him stride across the waiting area toward us. He held himself tall and proud with a grin that stretched across the room. He threw down his duffel bag and we all hugged.

"Good flight, son?" Ted asked.

"Had to sit in a sling all the way so I'm stiff. But I don't care. Just glad to be home. Have you seen my baby?"

"No, we waited for you," I said.

Several hours later we arrived at the base hospital, parked the car, found the maternity ward, and rushed to Karen's room.

She rose carefully from her bed and hugged Casey while I snapped a picture. Then all eyes focused on the bassinet next to Karen's bed. Casey took two huge steps and gazed down at the small form wrapped in a blanket. She had a mass of straight dark hair and lovely olive skin.

He stood motionless. I remember the quiet.

"You can pick her up, Babe," Karen chuckled. "Go ahead, she won't break."

"I know," he said in a solemn tone, but still didn't touch her.

Why the hesitation, I wondered?

Karen leaned over and impatiently picked her up and placed her in Casey's arms. My son and his child, what a wondrous sight. All the troubles of the past months seemed to melt away.

I snapped pictures: mother and child, father and child, all of them together, recorded for posterity. Ted and I cuddled Lisa, examining her little hands and feet, so tiny.

"We're grandparents! How about that," Ted said. I hadn't seen that sort of wondrous look on his face since we first saw Gina and Casey.

The hospital delayed Karen and Lisa's release a few more days making certain Lisa was addiction free. Then Casey took his little family to his in-law's home. We all gathered there for the afternoon and watched a video of the happy event, hours and hours of labor and finally the birth—the next best thing to being there, I supposed. Our families were actually compatible for one entire afternoon.

One Sunday night Casey and Karen came over for dinner. They left Lisa with her parents. They seemed so carefree it was a pleasure to be with them. After dinner we sat around the table and talked. For some reason I found myself telling the special stories of Gina's and Casey's adoptions. Of course, Gina had heard her story many times but Casey had never been interested in the fact that he was adopted, much less knowing the details. He was fascinated and listened to every word. And no one had to insist on the telling—I loved doing it.

"Gina was almost three-years-old when your dad and I decided we wanted another child. I felt that my life was too centered on Gina, but knew I certainly had a lot more love to give, we both felt that way. Did I call the attorney or did you, honey?"

"You did," Ted answered, "and he said he had three cases we might select from. Go on, you tell it."

"OK. So, a few days later a folder arrived in the mail and after reading about the three available babies, Dad and I talked about them. I just didn't feel that any of them was our child. I called the attorney and told him. He said, `Well, there is one unusual case. A woman is expecting a baby in March but her husband refuses to let her keep it because the father is another man.' Then he asked if this case interested us. Without any hesitation I told him that was our baby."

Casey grinned from ear to ear when I said this. He knew then, without a doubt, how much he was wanted and was really singled out from other babies.

"On March 31," I continued, "the attorney called to say you had arrived that afternoon and that he was on his way to get the papers signed. We had to leave you in the hospital for three days, rules, you know. And the night we went after you is a story in itself. Do you want to tell this part, honey?"

"No," Ted said, grinning, "you're on a roll. Go on."

"The attorney told us to come to the hospital Friday night at seven o'clock. He said, 'Bring a plain cloth diaper, a gown, and a plain blanket in an unmarked paper sack. This protects you from being identified by the nurses. Park in the far south corner of the parking lot. I'll meet you there.'

"Sure enough, he was there on the dot, took the sack and said he'd be back in a little while. It seemed forever, but about thirty minutes later he returned carrying you. I quickly opened the car door and he placed you in my arms. You were sound asleep and totally beautiful." I guess my voice cracked and we were all misty eyed at that point.

"Wow," Casey said leaning back in his chair.

Gina leaned over and rubbed his cropped hair, chuckled, and said, "Well, I remember very well how bald you were. Not a single hair on your head. We didn't think you'd ever have hair. Now look at you! Of course, the army won't let it grow out anymore."

We all laughed, then Ted said, "First things I noticed were your broad shoulders, barrel chest, and your white skin. Your mother said she was afraid you'd never be able to be in the sun. That changed, too."

"I thought with those shoulders and big chest you'd have to be good in sports. And I was right," I said.

"Either that or big winded," Casey said, pounding his chest. "Go on with the story, Mom."

"OK, let's see, where was I? Oh, yes, still in the parking lot at the hospital. First thing we did was to take you to see Emogene. Remember her, Casey?"

Casey and Gina both shook their heads, "She always had toys for us to play with," Gina said.

And Casey added, "Yeah, and she had that funny little black and white dog. And was always drinking Cokes."

"She was my closest friend in those days. Anyway," I went on, "we went back to Sue's house where we had left Gina. Sue, Bill, and their little girl oohed and aahed over you, and Gina's eyes were big as saucers over her little brother. And after a while we took you home. And that, my dear, is your story."

No one said a word. I glanced around the table. I marveled that Karen had paid such rapt attention. Without any drugs in her she was quite calm. Casey's face held a look of satisfaction. A lovely atmosphere of oneness and peace surrounded us all. It was a treasured moment after so much chaos.

Not long after Casey returned to the base, we received a letter from him.

It read:

Dear Mom and Dad,

Thank you for the opportunity to come home to see Lisa and to see you. Karen and I were talking about how much we enjoyed that evening with you guys. That was the best night I've had in a long time. To think I never knew about what it took for you to adopt the both of us. But I'm sure glad you did!

It seems that all my mistakes are crashing down on me now. I figure if I can quit the drugs then I can accomplish anything. Sometimes it feels like it is getting harder and harder to keep my head above water. I can't wait till I get back to level ground. I have the DWI payment, the bad checks, and when I get home, the bankruptcy. It sure is a big load to carry around. I need to hear your advice about how to take care of everything. I'm think I'm finally ready to listen.

Please send some pictures of the baby. It's hard being here all alone. Well, I guess that's it for now. And thanks again for that Sunday night. It was nice, wasn't it?

Love you guys,

Casey

P.S. Don't forget to go see your granddaughter. OK?

During the following months I visited Karen and Lisa regularly, taking great pride and joy in cuddling my new granddaughter. Several times Ted and I took care of her while Karen went out to dinner with her family.

She was a good baby, I don't recall her crying much at

all. Sometimes I stared at her, determined to memorize every detail. Karen insisted the baby favored Karen's father. I couldn't detect a likeness to anyone. Perhaps her mouth was a bit like Karen's, small and bow-shaped, but beyond that, nothing. Casey was sandy haired, blue-eyed, and fair skinned. Yet, somehow, none of us dwelt on this inconsistency, choosing to be content with things as they were.

I gloried in my new role with Lisa, feeding her, changing diapers, watching her sleep, and holding her close when she cried. Sometimes I buried my face in her blanket, loving the smell of her, and the incredible softness of her skin. I visualized the years to come, seeing her grow and learn.

The day before Casey's discharge was final he called me. I barely recognized his voice. Coarse sounding words came from deep in the back of his throat. "Karen just called me, Mom. Lisa's not mine."

Silence. A long empty silence. Silence that screamed at me. "Not yours?" I stammered. "What do you mean not yours?"

"She says Ron's the father. He's a buddy of mine here on base." Silence again. "He's Mexican, Mom."

I couldn't speak and Casey was sobbing like a hurt child, spilling out the awful words. "You remember when I first saw Lisa and couldn't pick her up? I knew then she wasn't mine. I thought, my God, she looks like Ron. I've bugged Karen about it ever since and she finally admitted it today." His voice choked up.

"It's been hard keeping this inside. I can't talk any more. I'm heading home tomorrow. I'll call before I leave. I love you. Tell Dad I love him, too."

I mumbled something unintelligible. The dial tone sounded like an alarm going off in my head. I hung up but found no comfort in the dead stillness that followed. I sat by the phone for a long time, listening to my breath. A million things raced through my mind, anger most of all.

How could Karen do this to him, and of all times to tell him, the day before he leaves for home. I wanted to rush over to her house, slap her face, and yell awful things at her. But I sat still—going numb. Oh, dear God, I prayed, help us to get through this nightmare.

I remembered the night we sat around the dinner table telling the story of Casey's adoption. How could Karen sit there so calmly while I told about Casey's birth mother having him by a man other than her husband? The gaul. If the situation were not so tragic I could have laughed at the utter irony of it.

I don't know how long I sat there but little by little I became functional again. My throat was dry and I went into the kitchen to get a drink of water.

Then worry struck. Was Casey strong enough to handle this? Or would he bomb out on drugs again? Would he make it home safely or give up and disappear somewhere like he had in the past?

* * *

SUB CHAPTER EIGHT

When Karen told me she was pregnant I couldn't believe what I was hearing. I felt excited while hurting inside. There we were doing all those drugs and that poor baby didn't have a shot at life . . . my baby we were doing that to. Sometimes we cried ourselves to sleep.

I came home on leave after my surgery. It was Karen's eighth month. The place we went to for the drugs was not far from my folk's house. We had to call for an appointment once a day between five and ten o'clock at night. A lady and her son ran the place and the son took the appointments. The lady was about sixty or sixty-five years old. She had a room in the back of the house where she stayed all the time. That room was apparently her whole life, she never left it, never came outside, stayed in there dealing. On one wall she had a glass book case with pipes and all the paraphernalia needed to support the habit.

She always seemed happy to see us. Why wouldn't she be? She made a lot of money off of us. She kept a jar of aloe vera for Karen and would rub her stomach with it, "To prevent stretch marks," she said. Crazy how she could be so concerned about our baby yet keep us high. But now I know we were the crazy ones for doing it to ourselves.

In March I got a call from the Red Cross. "Private Harper," the lady said, "your wife had a baby girl."

I was excited with the news but then it struck me, why hadn't someone in the family called me? I called Karen's parents and Dan answered. "Did Karen have her baby?" I asked.

"Yeah," he said.

"Why in hell didn't you call me? You drink all my vodka but can't call me when my child is born." Who the hell did he think he was? "Dan, do you know what?"

"What?" he said.

"You're one dirty son of a bitch."

"Same to ya," he said and hung up the phone. His answer to everything on the phone was to hang up.

Man, by this time I was ready to kill. Little did I know things were just beginning to get bad.

I went straight to my captain. "My wife just had our baby and I need a leave to go home."

"No excuse," he replied to me.

"I don't think you heard me right, Sir," I said back to him.

"I heard you, Harper. You can't have leave because you're getting kicked."

Son of a bitch, what now? Think, Casey, think, I told myself. I thought about the chaplain, bet he'd know somebody upstairs who could give me a leave.

"Sir, sir, you gotta help me."

"What is it, son?" he asked me.

"My wife just had our baby and the captain won't give me a leave because I'm being kicked soon . . . " and on I went explaining what had happened. Man, did I feel uncomfortable. There I was being kicked out of the army because I was an addict, standing in a church begging a preacher to help me.

He leaned over his desk and wrote a note right there on the spot. It said, "Private Harper may have leave for up to ten days. Anything after ten days will be considered a favorable action. Chaplain Morris."

I didn't know what 'favorable action' meant but if it meant something good I would have asked for a better discharge instead of a leave.

I thanked the chaplain with all the gratitude I could muster and went back to my captain.

"Here, Sir," I said with a cocky smile on my face.

"Ok, Harper, you've got your leave, ten days, starting now." He glared at me with killer eyes so I got out of there real fast.

I was off like a shot to the air force base where I called my folks. Then I caught a hop to a base in California.

Mom and Dad picked me up and we went straight to the hospital. Strange thoughts raced around in my head. I realized I really didn't want to see Karen. I only wanted to see my baby.

When we got to Karen's room I looked at my baby and thought, holy shit, she looks like Ron . . . our really good, obviously too good, friend back in Colorado. Her skin and eyes were Mexican. No doubt about it. Right there I knew Ron was a dead man as soon as I got back to the base.

I was ashamed not to want to touch the child but everyone kept insisting. I had to keep my thoughts deep inside.

After I got back from leave I told my roommate about Ron. My new roommate had been a biker, was about thirty years old, and was being kicked out for statutory rape. Real tough guy. He pulled out his gun and said, "Come on, let's go take care of him."

I was so full of hate I went along with him thinking he was going to kill Ron. But when we got to Ron's house he handed me the gun and said, "He's all yours. Kill him."

I opened the car door, got out, cocked the gun, and walked to the front door. While I was ringing the door bell, killing Ron seemed like a good idea in theory, but could I actually kill him? I waited but no one answered the bell. All I could think of was thank you, God, thank you, God, I love you, I love you, I love you.

I got back in the car and never saw Ron again. At that point I'd had all I could take. No more army, no daughter, no wife. Karen said she didn't feel like being in a relationship anymore . . . she didn't feel like it. I was broke, everybody calling me for money.

And I felt like I was alone. Totally alone.

* * *

Chapter Nine

HOME AGAIN—HOME AGAIN

CASEY'S discharge was honorable under general conditions, much better than dishonorable yet still a disappointment. He was finished with the drug busts and the CID until the court trials began. Then he would be expected to return to Fort Carson to testify. That necessity made us all afraid for his safety. Secretly I hoped something would happen to get him out of it. But that was in the future sometime. Getting him home was the important thing for the moment.

"I'll be leaving tonight, Mom, on a bus. *On a bus*, can you believe it? It takes thirty hours to get home that way. And after I get home they'll send me $50 for travel time. The crazy thing is that air fare is the same as the bus plus the $50. Dumb."

"Not to mention that the flight would only be a couple hours, not thirty. I agree, it is dumb. Your dad says the army does things the hard way, but they have the say so right now." Why, oh why, I thought—it only added to his humili-ation. I had to wonder how much more he could take.

Casey called us once along the way to let us know he was all right. He said he would arrive around two o'clock the next morning and call us from the bus station so we could pick him up. He had decided not to live with Karen, unless they could work things out. I was surprised at this decision because before he left the base he said he still wanted to be with her. I wondered why he changed his mind but was glad he had.

A little after two o'clock the next morning he called and Ted went after him. It felt good having him home with us after all the junk we'd been through.

Ted went on to work later that morning and I waited for Casey to wake up. After he'd had a long sleep, I cooked him some breakfast, and did he eat!

"First food I've had since chow time at the base two days ago."

I was appalled and asked him why.

"No money. The sergeant who took me to the gate to catch the bus into Colorado Springs knew I was broke. He yelled at the guard on duty, `You mean you're going to send this soldier home without a cent in his pocket?' The guard said she had no control over the situation. The sergeant turned to me and said he couldn't watch me leave like that. He shook my hand and said, 'Good luck and take care of yourself.' Real nice guy."

"I can't help wondering where this kind soul was when you needed a friend the past few months."

"We talked sometimes but there wasn't anything he could do. The powers that be wouldn't let me do anything anyway."

"Tell me about your trip home." I had to change the subject.

"You're not going to like this but the guy sitting next to me had a bottle of vodka and when he found out I didn't have any money for food he gave me the vodka. Would

have been better if he'd given me some money instead, because all I did was drink it all. I passed out in the rest room
and somebody woke me up hours later and made me go back
to my seat. It was a miserable trip."

I put down my coffee cup and gazed through the pa-
tio doors to my serene back yard bathed in sunlight. "Of
all the people you could have sat with it had to be some
old man with free booze." Absurd. When Casey sent Karen
home from Colorado, she and her mother drove their
truck, and one of the first things Karen's father did was to
refuse to let Casey have it back. Since Casey had filed bankruptcy, her father took over the payments and used it in
his business. So Casey was afoot and rode the bus wherever he needed to go. Considering his past record with
cars and payments it was understandable that we didn't trust
him to drive one of our cars. And he accepted that decision without argument or any of the old charming ways of
persuasion.

Karen's mother and dad refused to let Casey see
Lisa, refused to let *us* see her. Why were we being pun-
ished, I wondered? Karen was the culprit. Punish *her*, I
raged. It was all so unfair. I felt cheated. A child we had
loved was now taken away. Quite honestly I must say that
knowing Lisa was not Casey's child changed my feeling
for her. Strange, too, because I really think I had loved
her, but self-preservation does funny things to one's
thinking. It was a pulling away, a withdrawal, an attempt
to put my feelings on hold so I wouldn't feel the pain
and be able to help Casey if I could. One of the lessons
I've learned is not to waste time worrying about circumstances over which I have no control. That situation was
one of those times.

"What's in the package, Mom?"

"It's from your Aunt Jane in Dallas, for the baby I'd

guess." I picked it up, sorry that I'd left it out where he could see it.

Casey snatched it out of my hands, opened it and found one of the cutest dresses I've ever seen. I started to pick it up to put back in the box but Casey grabbed it from me. "I'll take it over to Karen's." His voice was strained yet determined.

"Oh, no you won't," I snapped. "Jane sent it thinking Lisa is your child, but she isn't, not any more. Maybe we should ask Jane what she wants us to do with the gift." I was losing control, and I knew it. Casey was belligerent—impossible—unreasonable, and wouldn't let me have the package.

"I'm taking it, Mom. I want Lisa to have it."

"But I don't want *Karen* to have it. Don't you see?"

No, he didn't see what I meant. He obviously didn't want to reason it out at all. Perhaps he couldn't let go of Lisa just yet.

His mind was made up about the gift, and off he went with it. I could only stand at my front door, watching him go, feeling helpless again.

I ached for my son, for his despair and bewilderment, and was filled with such longing for Lisa I wanted to howl. I needed to hold her once more, bask in her crooked smile, drown in her soft chocolate eyes, and have her little fingers curl around mine.

Walking on the beach one afternoon I took a lesson from the sea. Whipped cream clouds floated above in a sky too blue for words, and sea gulls dove and squawked in constant motion. The lesson I glimpsed was in the ceaseless, inevitable return of the waves to the shore, lapping up footprints, filling in trenches. It was the promise of continuity.

For several months after I retired from advertising sales, I wondered what to do with my time, I'd always been busy and needed to feel useful. Before Casey's return home,

I became interested in prison volunteer work which involved one-to-one interviews with inmates as a chaplain representative from my church.

Failure with Casey nagged at me even though I knew Ted and I had done the best we could under the circumstances. Still, failure as a mother was an ever recurring thought. Working with inmates seemed a way to pacify these feelings. Being able to help another mother's child might make all the heartache bearable. I knew I could relate to the problems of addiction.

I made application to my church, attended orientation classes at Donovan State Prison, a workshop at San Diego Prison Ministries, and obtained the necessary clearances.

This work was all I'd hoped it would be. Most of the people I visited had committed crimes associated with drug and alcohol abuse. Looking into their troubled eyes I saw hopeless, lonely, confused, lost children. No matter what the age was they seemed children to me. As time passed and I could see evidence of reform after a few of them were released, I realized that anyone can change. Wanting change more than anything else was necessary, though, and knowing someone cared about them.

I began to understand the world they came from: abuses of all kinds, families that were too busy to care, lack of morals and ethics in a society where these values have declined. Self-worth and self-esteem were most needed and I prayed to open eyes and hearts to possibilities for good.

I think Casey was proud of what I was doing because his friends would mention it to me and ask questions. Most of all I was proud, no, proud is not the right word, *grateful* to be of some value. And I knew if I helped just one person, I wouldn't feel like a failure anymore.

* * *

SUB CHAPTER NINE

It took ten months to process me out of the army. If they wanted me out so bad why did it take so long? After I was finished with the CID they figured they had to get me out of there fast because of the threats my ex-roommate made after the first drug bust. They couldn't guarantee my safety in the barracks so they pushed the paperwork through. It took only two days of out-processing to finalize the discharge after they decided they were through with me.

A sergeant was assigned to take me to get my out-pay. I don't remember his name but he was a nice guy. The lady on duty said, "Looks like you owe us some money."

My chin dropped and I said, "But I thought I'd get about fifteen hundred dollars." I couldn't believe my ears. "I don't have any money. How am I going to eat on the trip home?"

"Nothing I can do," she said with a shrug. I don't think she cared.

The sergeant glared at her. "This man has been in the United States army and now you are sending him on a bus ride all the way to California with no money? What the hell is he supposed to eat? He is still a soldier for thirty-six hours after he leaves this base. He deserves better than this, don't you agree?"

The lady looked a little spooked but again said she couldn't do anything about it. She explained my pay was being held against the money I had borrowed.

We both stormed off angry at the system. That sergeant stood up for me yet didn't even know me or anything about me. Admirable, I thought.

I told a friend in the barracks what had happened.

"I can't believe they're treating you this way. Not right. How about if I loan you twenty?"

He knew I would never pay it back but offered anyway. It

seemed to me now that people all around me were changing because I was leaving. Had I made an impact on their lives, good or bad? It didn't matter as long as I had made a difference.

My squad leader, Sergeant Taylor, volunteered to take me outside of the post the next day. When we got to the gate he stuck out his hand for a final handshake, "Well, this is it," he said.

Another shocker. "What do you mean?"

"I have to drop you off out here. And I have to tell you that you can never return to Fort Carson as long as you live."

Sounded like the voice of doom reciting rules. I couldn't believe what I was hearing. "Sarge, you can't just leave me here. How will I get to the bus station?"

I don't know what he expected me to do. Maybe he thought I'd just turn and walk away like a good little soldier. I threw down my duffle bag and I guess my face was ten shades of red.

"Well," he said, like an apology, "Maybe I could take you somewhere."

"I know a girl that lives not far from here. Could you take me there?"

He agreed and off we went. I spent the next few days with the girl. I really liked her and promised I'd come back for her. She knew better, and so did I. I could tell by the look in her eyes when she dropped me off at the bus station. I was sad about leaving her. She was a nice girl, but I was on my way home. Nothing else seemed to matter.

It took me a while to realize I was no longer a soldier. No more reporting for duty. It was over.

Somewhere in El Paso, Texas a long haired guy got on the bus and sat next to me. Rick was his name. "Where you comin' from?"

"Just got out of the army."

"Right on!" he said.

We talked a while then he said, "Looks like we'll be stoppin' soon to eat. Come on with me."

"Can't. No money."

"Well, to hell with eatin'. Let's get drunk."

Sounded like a fine idea to me. I could forget all my troubles.

After the bus stopped we went across the street and Rick got two bottles of vodka and a gallon of orange juice.

After a while, and too much to drink, I went to the rest room and passed out. Four hours later I heard, "Wake up. Wake up," from Rick. Took me a while but I finally came to. I felt awful. Couldn't believe how long I'd been out. Didn't anyone else on the bus need to go for that four hours?

I started to light a cigarette but the bus driver yelled at me, "We're in California now. Can't smoke on the bus."

Stupid rule, I thought. I needed that cigarette.

When Rick got off the bus in L.A. he gave me his telephone number and I thanked him for a hell of a ride. He laughed and went on his way. Last time I ever saw him—probably a good thing.

The bus took off for Oceanside. I was almost home but some-how felt my life was over. I could have died on that bus for all I cared.

Oceanside was where it had all started thirty months ago to the day. Strange. Had it been real or was it all a dream? I honestly don't think I knew what was real anymore.

I looked out of the window and saw Dad. What a relief it was to see him. I had put this man through hell, but he was still there for me. We hugged for a long time and it felt good.

"Come on, son," he said. "Let's go home."

✳ ✳ ✳

Chapter Ten

FROM THE BOTTOM LOOKING UP

CASEY was restless, but I could see a change in him, a quietness never there before. Considering his humiliation in the army this was understandable.

He wasted no time finding a job with the aid of an employment agency. His first job was with a plumbing contracting company and he stayed there for about six months. Then he was offered a better opportunity to work for an electronics firm where he has remained. His supervisor at the first place was a recovering alcoholic and they became friends. During one discussion about AA Casey asked, "Tell me about AA. What do I do to get in?"

"Well, son, you go to hell first, then make a U-turn." The supervisor grinned.

Casey chuckled and said, "I've been in hell for a long time already."

When he told me about this later he shook his head saying, "Hell was easy. It's the U-turn that's gonna be hard."

Aftereffects from his surgery lingered for a long time, over a year. He had pain frequently and had to be careful about what he ate. Soon after his return home the stitches opened up and he had to have that taken care of at Pendleton Base Hospital. Ted and I were concerned about his health since we didn't know if he was staying off the drugs.

One night, several weeks after our conversation about AA, he handed me some sheets from a legal pad and asked me to read what he'd written. I was impressed that he'd taken time to write down what had been happening in his life. I remembered other things he'd written before the army, songs mostly, with words of deep despair.

After he left for work, I settled down to read his latest thoughts:

"I decided to go to an AA meeting one night and wondered if I had the courage to go. Feeling shaky, I went to a bar down the street from the meeting place and got drunk first. Finally, I walked through the doors to the meeting. After I'd been there a while I found out it takes more courage to stay. I couldn't wait for it to be over so I could go have another beer. But to my surprise I was invited out to dinner with some of the people from the fellowship. I realized I didn't have to drink anymore that night. But what about tomorrow?

The next day came and I had a choice to make. At that time I didn't know anything about the higher power referred to in AA, a higher power that could help me make choices. Of course, I knew about God because I'd been to Sunday School growing up, but in AA God is called a higher power. Anyway, I had to make a decision about whether to go back to AA again. I chose to go instead of drinking that night.

Karen's sister, Joyce, was in the program and she

helped me a lot. She had been through three or four rehab programs and had served time in prison, but today she was sober. I thought that was a real miracle. I really didn't know how she'd done it but I knew she had what I wanted. I wanted to be able to smile, have friends, be honest, love again, and have a warm heart.

Joyce's boyfriend, Bill, was also in the program and had been sober for eight years. He's about forty-five with grown kids. He told me, "Go to the meetings and find somebody who can kick your ass then ask him to be your sponsor."

Well, I sat through the meetings but didn't see anyone I thought could do it. One night I got in Bill's truck and rode with him to the restaurant where we all went after the meetings.

"Did you find anyone to be your sponsor?" he asked.

"Nobody I thought could kick my ass."

He laughed, and I was confused about the whole thing. We became good friends and I started to trust him. After all, he'd been where I'd been, on the bottom. One night I asked him to be my sponsor, he accepted, and sobriety for me was ready to begin.

It's been hard as hell but I am learning to turn everything over to God. I just pedal like crazy and He has the handlebars."

Happy tears rolled down my cheeks and splashed on Casey's words. After praying for such a long time here was an answer. Whatever works, I told myself, whatever works is fine.

If Joyce could find her way to AA, I couldn't help wondering why Karen was still struggling with addiction. But we all have choices to make. I guess she wasn't ready for a better way. Too bad.

* * *

SUB CHAPTER TEN

I was finally out of the army and home again. Now what, I wondered. No more free food and housing. No more job. What the hell was I going to do with my life, such as it was. Everything that meant anything to me was gone.

Somehow or other I wasn't thinking about doing drugs. Since I didn't consider myself an alcoholic I was still drinking and thought that was OK.

The first thing I decided to do was file bankruptcy since I was so deep in debt. Had to wipe the slate clean and start over. So I found myself a lawyer and went to his office. While I was there would you believe my sister-in-law, Joyce, came in. She had the same lawyer.

She looked me right in the eyes and said, "Casey, what you need is to go to an AA meeting."

Funny, here was the same girl who taught me about drugs, how to shoplift and deal for drug money, telling me to go to an AA meeting. The last time I went to a meeting with her it was to the bathroom to shoot up. I didn't promise anything, told her I'd think about it. The change in her appearance got my attention right away. Before she looked like any other druggy, thin and strung out. But there she was looking fresh and alive, a new person.

After I got home I thought maybe going wasn't such a bad idea. I called AA and found out there was a place in Leucadia called Step House and the next meeting was at eight o'clock. Since I didn't have a car I went everywhere on the bus. It wasn't far since Leucadia is a little town that's part of Encinitas. I got there about an hour too early though, and thought, what the hell will I do until eight.

I looked around and guess what I saw, that's right, a

bar. So off I went. I walked in and sat down by some guys. They bought me drinks to celebrate my army discharge. Next thing I knew I was feeling pretty good. "I'm going to an AA meeting down the street. Wanta go with me?" I said.

"Sure," they said.

So off we stumbled in a drunken stupor to AA.

That's where I met Bill, Joyce's boy friend, a tough man, eight years sober. He wasn't a very big guy but was trim and muscular from doing construction work. He had black bushy hair with lots of gray in it and a beard. As time went by he turned out to be a good friend and I owe him a lot.

I started growing in a good way then, and hopefully, always will be. I realized we take too much for granted in this hustle bustle world of ours.

* * *

Chapter Eleven

STUMBLES AND STARTS

MOST of Casey's first pay checks went to the employment agency. After about four weeks he was able to keep his entire check and we expected him to come by the house after work as he usually did on payday. This happened on a Friday and after he cashed his check he went up to San Marcos to Gina's place to spend the week-end dog-sitting while she was out of town. We worried because we didn't hear from him that night. Casey never could handle having money in his pocket. He called the next morning around ten o'clock. I had to pull the words out of him. "I spent my pay check last night on drugs," he said in a low guttural voice that sounded like somebody I didn't know.

"You spent it all?" I shrieked at him.

"All of it."

"You idiot," I said, and wasn't proud of calling him that. "Where are you?"

"At Bill's."

"I'll be right there."

I flew out of the door and was there in five minutes. I should have called Ted but was in too much of a hurry to think about that before I left.

Casey was waiting at the curb in front of Bill's house. He opened the door and got in. He looked so sad—drooping shoulders and red eyes. His words rushed out like saying them would make everything better. "I spent the whole check, Mom. I swear I didn't mean to do it. I cashed my check, went to Gina's, and fixed myself some dinner. Then I wanted some ice cream.

"So I got in my car and before I knew it I had driven to Oceanside to a place where I knew they sold crack. I was walking back to my car with $400 worth of it in my hands before what I had done hit me. I drove back to Gina's and did it all. Just bombed out." I stared at him like I didn't know him, feeling angry and sick. I finally mumbled, "Are you all right now?"

"I'm OK."

We grabbed each other and hugged tightly, not wanting to let go, both of us crying.

"I don't ever want to go through anything like this again. I swear I don't," he sobbed into my hair.

"What is it you say in AA? One step at a time?"

"One day at a time. Today I'm sober."

"You know what I think?" I said, trying to be optimistic. "I think you're going to be all right."

He didn't answer.

Joyce came outside and asked, "Are you guys OK?"

"We're fine," I said glancing at Casey.

We got out of the car and Casey said, "I'm going inside, Mom." Turning toward the front door of the house he added, "I'll see you later. Are you going to tell Dad?"

"Don't you think I should?"

"I guess so," he said.

"I've kept too much from him already. All that business with Western Union—he didn't know about that for a long time. I've always kept things about you from him, to protect you, I thought. But it didn't do you any good at all. No more secrets from now on. You can trust him. He loves you very much, you know."

He managed a slight yet sad smile before he turned away and went in the house.

AA became a way of life for Casey. He went to a meeting almost every night. Late one night a girl he'd met at AA called and said she had to have a drink and needed to go a meeting and would he take her. Before he left he said he was glad to do it because it was time for him to help someone else if he could.

A safety plan for Casey's pay checks was arranged. He gave us his uncashed checks and we became his banker. We gave him $20 at a time, a sum he felt he could safely handle. We loaned him $4000 for a used car and took the payments and insurance out of his pay. This proved to be a good plan. To our delight, he kept up the payments and finally proved himself trustworthy.

He met a girl named Ria at AA. She was a full-blooded Indian girl, shy and hard to know. Casey told me that one night, before she stopped drinking, she had a car crash and was in a coma for a month. When she woke up she learned her vocal cords had been severed and she could only speak in a coarse whisper. Several months later she started going to AA and had been sober five years.

Before very long she and Casey decided to live together and moved into their own place south of San Diego, in Imperial Beach. Ted and I were not thrilled about this arrangement, but had to learn to accept what was best for Casey. We also had to learn to trust his judgement. We did recognize the fact that Ria was the best support system he could have at that point and were grateful for her.

He enrolled in a computer college and applied for student loans. About two years later, when his car was paid for, he assumed responsibility for handling his pay checks. We were shaky about it and were still learning to trust him. He made some mistakes managing money by himself but nothing crucial.

The CID called several times from Fort Carson to make arrangements for Casey to return to testify at the drug trials. Casey was at work each time they called and they never called again. We considered it a closed book and were relieved.

Karen filed for divorce about six months after his discharge. She filed so Casey wouldn't be required to pay child support—as if he would! He learned she was living with a fellow she'd met at AA and was drawing child welfare. So like her. Still a user.

After the decree was final we hoped we'd seen the last of her, but it wasn't long before she popped up again with another little surprise.

* * *

SUB CHAPTER ELEVEN

In AA sobriety dates are marked by tokens. The first thirty days earns a token, then sixty, ninety, one year, and so on. On May 10, 1989 I earned my first. Sober thirty days. Hard to believe I did it. But hard doesn't describe what it's like to make it through each day. But I did what AA says to do and went to a meeting every night and called my sponsor when I felt the urge to drink or do drugs again.

After thirty-six days of sobriety, my pay check was mine to keep without giving any to the employment agency, so I cashed it and had $440 in my hand. Funny thing, though, the thought of getting high never crossed my mind.

I drove to Gina's house, cooked myself some dinner, and a little later, I wanted some frozen yogurt and needed to put some gas in my car. When I got to the yogurt shop I didn't stop, kept going about twelve miles to Oceanside. I had never bought stuff there before, but for some reason knew exactly where to go.

I crossed the main drag and drove down a dark street. A man was standing out there on the curb. I stared at him, he stared back, then raised his arm and motioned to me. I knew he had to be a dealer. He had that rawboned hungry look, black as the night, waiting for suckers to come his way. I pulled over next to where he stood.

"What can I get for you, my man?" He leaned against the car and crossed his long legs.

"Some rock."

"How much?"

"$400 worth."

This made him extremely happy. He grinned all over himself, knowing how much he was going to make off me. In the dim light, I saw a nasty looking scar on his right cheek that moved up and down when he spoke.

"Here take these and I'll be right back. Gotta make a phone call."

He handed me his pipe and some rock to smoke while he was gone. That was rare. Dealers don't usually give out their pipes.

That first draw felt good, I mean incredibly good. How can something so bad feel so good, I thought, and wondered how I got sober in the first place.

He came back to the car. "Let's go," he said, and we were off to the rock house. He sat sideways like he wanted to keep an eye on me. "You want white, black, or Oriental?"

I glanced at him, sitting there so full of himself. "What do you mean?"

"What kind of woman you want?"

"Woman?" I laughed. "All I want is the stuff. I don't want to pay for a woman, too."

"She's free with so much rock. Why wouldn't you want her?" he said, like I ought to know such a thing.

"Black, I guess," I said, without thinking about it. Why I said black, I don't know.

"Good choice," he said, patting my shoulder. The pat felt odd, like he was taking something out of me. "Here, stop here," he said, pointing to a house across the street.

I dug down in my jacket pocket for the money and handed it to him. He counted it and left. After about ten minutes, which seemed like a lifetime, I began to worry. Why should he bother coming back. I thought. He had my money in his greedy hand.

Sitting there with the dark night around me, I wondered what I was doing there. A cold blast of ocean breeze stung my eyes. I shivered and zipped up my jacket. Fingers of smoky fog reached through the trees and I heard a dog barking like he had something cornered.

Pretty soon the man came back with a black girl. In this business people get ripped off all the time, yet there he was, like he said. "Enjoy," he said with a sly toothy grin as he ambled away.

I took the girl back to Gina's house and spent the night with rock and sex. We did the whole $400 worth. What a night that was.

Next morning, I drove her back to the rock house, and you know, it's funny, I don't remember a single thing about her, not even her name.

After I dropped her off, that's when I realized what I had done. It was like a nightmare and I was still in it. My stomach churned and I felt sick. How dumb can I be, always jumping in without thinking things through? Then I thought about Bill. Another dumb thing. Supposed to think about my sponsor before I get the drugs, not after. Better call him.

"Come on over here," he said in a low somber voice, like somebody died.

Man, I dreaded seeing him.

When I got to his house people were all over the place. "What's going on?" I asked.

"We're celebrating my eighth AA birthday. Stay and have lunch. All these guys are AA, so you're in good company. And try to settle down, you still look wired."

That was all I needed, being high as a kite, depressed, hanging around sober people all day. But I guess I had no where else to go.

Bill's girl friend, Joyce, passed by, grabbed my arm, and smiled that deep self-satisfied grin that said how happy she was with herself.

I thought a lot of her. She had been on drugs ten, maybe twelve years. Got in trouble on a federal charge and spent two years up in an Orange County prison. Yet here she was, clean and sober two years.

"Better call your folks," she said.

"You people are big on spilling your guts, aren't you? Telling my folks what I've done this time is the last thing I want to do."

"You could practice on me if you want to. Come on."

We found a quiet corner in the living room, and settled down on the sofa. She sat sideways facing me, with her long legs tucked up under her. I sat in the middle, looking straight ahead, fumbling with my hands.

"I guess the first mistake I made was cashing my check after work. I was supposed to take it to Dad. He's been giving me an allowance just so something like this wouldn't happen. I got in my car after dinner to get some frozen yogurt, for god's sake. Next thing I know, I'm sitting up in Oceanside waiting for crack.

"How can I possibly explain this to my folks? I can already hear the fight we'll have, like we always do when I screw up. Dad's the one I'm afraid of. He never hits me or anything like that, just yells a lot." *I felt like a fool, crying like a baby, but it did help to get it all out.*

"Go ahead and cry," *Joyce said.* *"Have a good one. I used to cry all day. You'd better call. I think you're ready now."*

I got up, went in the kitchen, and dialed home. Mom an-

swered, Dad was at work, thank God. I sort of made her guess what was going on and she figured it out right away.

"You idiot," she said.

I couldn't blame her, I'd done a stupid thing. I'd put them both through hell. OK, so I wasn't what she wanted me to be. I was an addict. That was apparently what I did best.

When Mom drove up in front of Bill's house, I was on the curb waiting. I got in the car and could see what I had done to her. It was dead quiet.

Finally, she said, I wish I could understand. No, I guess I don't. I'd have to be in your shoes to do that."

And she was right. I respected her for not giving me a lecture, for being so quiet. That was an important day for me. I was face to face with my parent, talking about drugs. I told her the whole story.

She listened, staring ahead through the windshield, squinting from the glare of bright morning sunshine. A clumsy bumblebee crawled around on the wipers, then flew away. People passed by, and yet, it was like we were isolated, in a world apart.

"I'm sorry I called you an idiot," she said, taking my shaky hand. "Your eyes are so red. Are you all right?"

"I'm OK." I saw the hurt and anger in her eyes.

They looked like the ocean, soft blue and distant.

We grabbed each other, holding on, not wanting to let go, both of us crying.

"I swear I don't know why I did it. I just bombed out."

Mom held me tight, saying nothing. I could almost feel the anger draining out of her.

"I don't ever want to go through anything like this again. I swear I don't." I sobbed like a baby into her soft silvery hair.

"What is it you say in AA? One step at a time?"

"One day at a time. Today I'm sober."

"You know what I think?" Mom said, pushing away, gazing into my eyes. "I think you're going to be all right."

I couldn't answer.

Joyce came outside, slamming the front door behind her. "Are you guys OK?" she said, leaning over, looking into the car.

"We're fine," Mom said, her eyes still fastened on mine, studying my face, like she was trying to read my thoughts.

We got out of the car and walked to the door. Joyce hugged me and went inside.

I turned to face Mom. "Are you going to tell Dad?"

"Don't you think I should?" she said, crossing her arms.

I shuddered at the thought. Dad was always mad at me anyway. I never did anything right, according to him. Deep inside I wished I could be what he wanted his son to be, to make him proud.

"I've always kept things about you from him, to protect you, I thought. But it just made things worse. No more secrets from now on. You can trust him, he loves you very much, you know."

She hugged me again, standing on her tip toes to put her arms around me. "Come home when you can," she said.

I tried to smile, but felt sad, drained. I shuddered again like an icy wind had hit me. The high was wearing off. I watched Mom walk slowly to her car, and wave as she drove away.

One thing for sure, I realized at that moment. I have to stop blaming everybody else for what I do. I must be responsible for myself.

In AA, it is said, an addict will keep going back again and again for that next fix or that next drink until he is done. For the first time I knew what that meant. I was done. I could feel it. In my head and in my heart, I knew it was over.

* * *

Chapter Twelve

STILL A USER

CASEY called me around noon one day and I could hear the shock and disbelief in his voice.

"Guess what Karen's done this time?"

"I can't imagine," I replied. "Should I sit down?" I heard a sinister little snicker as he answered.

"You remember I told you she's drawing child welfare. I just found out it's over $500 a month. A man from the D.A.'s office was here this morning to serve lawsuit papers. The county is *suing me* for the money they've paid *her*. Can you believe it?"

"Well, I guess with Karen anything is possible. You mean an officer came to see you at work? I think that's awful."

"He didn't have on a uniform or anything. Just an ordinary little man in a brown suit. He was nice, seemed almost sorry he had to do it. He said I can get a public defender when I go to the hearing. Won't cost me anything."

"Good. Lawyers can be expensive. Did he give you a court date?"

"October 19. The suit is for $10,000! Where am I going to get that kind of money?"

"In the first place Lisa isn't yours and you can prove it. It'll work out, I'm sure of it. Just tell the attorney exactly what happened."

Good grief, I thought, hanging up the phone. Karen again.

Ted and I met Casey and Ria at the court house on October 19 and waited in the lobby while Casey talked to a public defender.

About an hour later we went into the court room, which was smaller than I had imagined. About seventy-five percent of the space was for the judge's bench, lawyer's desks, and file cabinets. The rest of the space was for spectators. About forty people tried to crowd into twenty-five seats. The rest of us lined the walls and stood in the doorway.

It was stuffy, smelling of sweaty, tobaccoed bodies. Three or four times a wiry little ill-tempered lady pushed her way through us and snapped, "You people can't block this door." But we all laughed at that weird lady and stayed right where we were, not having any place else to stand.

In about thirty minutes the judge arrived and the hearings began. Casey's was fourth on the docket.

The case was read and Casey's lawyer said, "The defendant is denying paternity, your honor, and we would like a continuance."

"Granted," the judge said. "Hearing is set for November 19."

Quick, crisp, and to the point.

Casey was not satisfied with the public defender's nonchalant attitude so he decided to hire an attorney if he could find a cheap one. Which he did, through a buddy in

AA. The fee was $500 to handle the case and since Casey didn't have any money we loaned it to him. Good old Mom and Dad, Gina said.

Sometimes I wonder if parents ever have a reprieve from parenting, if we could possibly raise our children and at a certain age send them off to their own responsible lives. Birds and animals do it. Where did we humans go wrong in the scheme of things?

Our involvement in Casey's life was certainly not at an end, by any means. But then, I suppose there is much to be said for being needed.

Karen I could do without easily. This little scam of hers was the last straw. Granted, she wasn't the one suing Casey, but her greed certainly was the reason behind it. I raged within like a furnace about to explode. Mentally I called the welfare office and reported her as an imposter. She surely wasn't destitute because she and Lisa were living with a man she had met at AA who supported them, and she had her family as well. The thought of my tax money going to her galled me.

But I held my tongue, for only one reason. I was certain that someday she will get her just desserts and I won't have to be the one to do it. She'll trip herself up.

November rolled around quickly and we were in court again. Casey's case was read and the judge said, "Mr. Harper, do you have a copy of your divorce decree?"

Casey replied, "No sir," and shot a questioning look at his attorney. "Why do we need it?" he whispered to him.

The judge picked up some papers from his desk and said, "I have a copy and it seems your wife made no mention of a child in her divorce petition. I'll set a continuance for proof of paternity. In the meantime, you, your wife, and the child will have blood tests. Court date is set for February 19."

A sharp rap of the gavel and the session was over.

Casey's attorney grinned at Casey. "What a stroke of

luck Karen didn't declare the child. Here's the address for
the blood test. And it's free. The county pays for it."

Casey smiled at us. One more hurdle overcome, thank
goodness.

Several weeks later Casey went to the clinic in east San
Diego for the blood test. When he called me later he was
laughing. "Would you believe that Karen and Lisa were at
the clinic when I got there? Wonder what the odds are of
that happening on the same day?"

"Did she have much to say?"

"She seemed a little quieter than usual. Guess she was
afraid I was mad at her. Sometimes I wish I could just haul
off and let her have it. Don't think I'd feel any better,
though. Not my style."

And thank God for that, I thought.

The first week in January, Casey received a letter from
his attorney. The blood tests had proved his case and the
lawsuit was dropped.

"Wouldn't it be nice if we could get the $500 attorney
fee from Karen? She could sign over one of her welfare
checks to you. It seems to me she should be made to pay
for something in this life, just once." Casey picked up on
my resentment right away. "I'm so tired of being mad at
her, Mom. But I'd just as soon drop it. Besides, there's no
way I could get any money from her. It's over as far as I'm
concerned. I'll pay you back myself as soon as I'm able."

"What about Lisa? How do you feel about her?" I had
avoided this question for a long time thinking it might
upset him, but it popped out unexpectedly.

"You know," he said with a calmness in his voice I'd
never heard before, "once I got sober it was OK. I was
ready to get on with my life."

I didn't answer. I understood. And I realized if he could
let go then I should be willing to do the same.

Remembering his words later, I recalled an incident I

had tucked away deep inside me, like a memento to be brought out and savored. Casey had called me one day from Bill's house. His AA group was having a celebration of some kind and he asked if I could come over for a little while. Since I hadn't seen him for a week or so, I readily agreed.

Another telephone call delayed my leaving and by the time I arrived at Bill's house, Karen and Lisa had joined the group. When I walked into the kitchen and saw them Karen and I were silent at first. Seeing Lisa in her arms, I went over and asked, "May I hold her?"

"Sure," she replied, handing Lisa to me.

"Hello, sweetheart, how's my girl," I said hugging her. She smiled at me, although I am certain she didn't recognize me. It had been too long since I had seen her. I sat her down facing me on the side of the butcher block table in the center of the room. She dangled her tiny feet over the edge. Her Mary Jane shoes reminded me of Gina when she was a little girl. "I love your dress. Blue must be your best color."

"That's the dress Ted's sister sent from Dallas: I guess it's one of my favorites," Karen said.

"Well, I'm glad I got to see it on her." I stroked Lisa's straight hair, picked her up, and hugged her again. "Thanks, Karen, for letting me hold her. Are you getting along all right?" I said handing Lisa back to her.

I think she replied, "OK" but I recall vividly that I turned and walked away and didn't look back. I had let Lisa go and didn't realize it until after Casey said what he did about getting on with his life. And so was I. Hooray!

* * *

SUB CHAPTER TWELVE

Letting go seems and sounds relatively easy. It is if you have a total understanding of your higher power. When I was a kid going to Sunday School I learned that God is all-seeing, all-acting, and all-wise, among many other wonderful things. To know God is to love Him.

I have learned that if I want God to show me the way I have to let Him. My own will trips me up though, then I turn around and blame everything on Him. He probably sits up there and laughs when He sees me stumbling all over the place.

Having the right tools is what is needed, and I have them but use substitutes sometimes. Always gets me into trouble. Like using a crescent wrench instead of a socket or ratchet. Smash my fingers something awful. Like drowning myself with booze or drugs, those are the substitutes. Now when I have a problem I see it as something God can deal with if I let Him. Isn't that nice?

I should say so. If He has to take me by the hand and lead me around like a little child I let Him. I won't fall. I'm not preaching all this, just sharing what I've learned. It works for me.

One of my instructors at Coleman College was in AA, seven years sober when I knew him. He gave me this poem:

> *LET GO . . . LET GOD*
> *(Sometimes called: Broken Toys, Broken Dreams)*
> *As children bring their broken toys*
> *with tears for us to mend,*
> *I brought my broken dreams to God*
> *because He was my friend—*
> *But then, instead of leaving Him*
> *in peace to work alone . . .*
> *I hung around and tried to help*
> *with ways that were my own.*

At last I snatched them back and
cried, "How could you be so slow?"
"My Child," He said, "what could I
do? You never did let go . . ."

* * *

Chapter Thirteen

ON HIS WAY

THE air in the crowded room was thick with tobacco smoke and the aroma of brewing coffee. About twenty-five men and women stood around in groups, talking quietly. They were all shapes, sizes, and races. Some were neatly dressed, some weren't. A few of them had a withdrawn attitude, not looking anyone squarely in the face, keeping secrets. Others joked about hunger, prisons, and being at the bottom of the human heap.

This was my first AA meeting. It was a momentous occasion and I tried to absorb it all so I wouldn't forget any detail. Haunted expressions in eyes and smiles tugged at my heart and filled my senses. Casey was foremost in my thought, though, and I was aware of where he was in the room, eying him proudly. He stood broad-shouldered and tall, like a man knowing who he was, confident and at peace with himself. His eyes were bright and clear, creased at the corners from the smile that reached across his tanned face while he spoke with his friends.

The meeting was in an old house called Step House near the beach. The lights were dim and the floor creaked underfoot. Casey told me later the members contributed money to pay the rent and operating expenses. The side door was wide open to let in the cool ocean breeze.

I listened, in awe, as a man standing in front of me laughed loudly, revealing large gaps where teeth once were. A long jagged scar on his left cheek witnessed his rough life.

"Seems funny standin' around drinkin' free coffee. Time was I stole water from toilets and slept in doorways, when I wasn't in jail, that is."

"Yeah, same here," the short bearded man next to him said. "I spent twelve years in San Quentin for killing a man over a bottle of beer. Man I wanted that beer. Staying alive was hard. Life's better now."

Casey waved to me and called out, "Come on over here, Mom. Bill and Joyce just came in."

"Hi, Anne," they said to me, and Joyce and I hugged. One thing I've noticed about the people at AA is that they hug and say "I love you" a lot. Every time I spoke to Casey he would end the conversation with, "I love you", and at one point when he wasn't doing too well with sobriety and still not telling us the truth about some things, I told him not to tell me he loved me until he could prove it. It could be that I wanted him to first love himself enough to change.

"Bill," Casey said, "Come meet my dad and sister." He glanced at Ted and Gina. "Bill is my sponsor I've told you about, and you already know Joyce."

Ted grabbed Bill's outstretched hand. "I'm glad to finally meet you. We appreciate what you've done more than you know," he said.

Casey and Bill exchanged grins, nice warm expressions, and I could see the respect they shared. Casey lowered his head, self-consciously, the way he did as a child.

"Time to get started," a raspy voice called out from across the room.

Casey pointed toward some chairs and said, "Mom, there'll be less smoke over near the door." He chuckled and moved away to sit by Ria. He enjoyed teasing, but I thought it was a considerate gesture since we were probably the only non-smokers in the place. Another thing I've noticed about people at AA is that they smoke and drink a great deal of coffee. "Hi, I'm Brian, and I'm an alcoholic," the raspy voice said. He continued, telling how AA works and reading the twelve steps to recovery.

Someone called out, "Any cakes and tokens tonight?"

Ria raised her hand. "This is my sixth token and Casey's first, and we brought a cake for him, too." A shy smile spread across her bronzed face. Sun bleached hair, pulled back with a ribbon, accented her high cheek bones. She accepted her token from Brian and in a coarse whisper, she said, "Well, all I can say is it gets easier if you stick with the program." After a short embarrassed pause, she added, "Thanks." We had to strain to hear her soft voice.

She rushed to the kitchen and brought back the cheese cake I had made for Casey. I had learned that the cake is symbolic, marking years like a birthday cake. Casey's AA birthday date was June 16, 1989.

"Stand up, Casey," Ria said while moving to his side. The members clapped in appreciation.

Casey stared at the token in his hand, cleared his throat, and said haltingly, "This is great. There were times I didn't think I'd make it." His voice cracked and he glanced up at us. "Since today is Father's Day this token is not just for me but for my dad, too." He strode quickly over to Ted, and pressed the token into his palm.

Tears rolled down my cheeks and I grabbed Ted's arm

and squeezed it. He didn't look up. I supposed he didn't trust himself to look at Casey for fear he'd cry like the rest of us. Any other time I would have been embarrassed to cry in front of strangers, but not then. We knew what that moment had cost Casey. He'd lived a lifetime in his twenty-five years.

I thought of the years leading up to that moment— the anger, frustration, tears, and heartache, wondering if he would survive—wondering if any of us would survive. At that moment, seeing him sober and in command of his life, it didn't matter what the future held. Recovery at best is fragile, I realized, but he'd made it this far. Anything was possible.

"May I see the token?" I asked Ted. It was bronze in color, about the size of a silver dollar. One side had a triangle with Unity printed along the left angle, Service on the right angle, and Recovery along the bottom line. Inside the triangle was a circle with the number one inside it, signifying how many years sober. Around the circle were the words, "To thine own self be true". The Serenity Prayer was on the other side of the token. I read the words, "God grant me the serenity to accept the things I cannot change, the courage to change the things I can, and the wisdom to know the difference."

Serenity, courage, wisdom. Had Casey found these yet, I wondered? Little by little I could see that these qualities were becoming evident in his character. Gazing at him through the smoky haze, a sense of freedom washed over me, the freedom to finally let him go and not spend every waking morning worrying about him. A dear friend once told me not to see him as he appeared to be. It was only a masquerade. The real Casey Harper was hidden underneath the mask. And now the man we knew he could be was beginning to emerge. He had made a crucial turn. He was on his way.

* * *

SUB CHAPTER THIRTEEN

Unbelievable! I had already earned thirty, sixty, and ninety day tokens and the night arrived for my one year award at Step House. It was Father's Day 1990. When my turn came to get my token, I had no idea what to say. It was important to let the newcomers know AA really works.

In the back of the room away from the smoke haze, I could see three familiar faces—Gina, Mom, and Dad. Looking in Dad's eyes, I saw what I yearned to see. He was proud, they all were, but he was the one I needed the most right then. I thought of all the years he must have been ashamed to talk about me to his friends. Now he had something to brag about.

When I said, "Happy Father's Day, Dad", I don't know how everyone reacted. I remember all I wanted to do was to hold him. After all the pain I had caused, I was finally creating pleasure. Not to take anything away from my sister and mom, I simply wanted to say thanks, Dad. Thanks for being there for me. Thanks for being my dad.

* * *

Chapter Fourteen

TOMORROW AND TOMORROW

"CASEY Harper," the president of Coleman Computer College called out.

The graduation ceremony took place in a large tent on a small hill directly behind the main building. About a hundred and fifty people were there facing a platform bathed in bright sunlight. An American flag hung in the center in back of the desk and microphone.

Casey strode briskly to where the president was standing at the foot of the platform steps. His black robe flowed in the warm afternoon breeze, the tassel on his cap swinging with every step. It was February 8, 1991. So much had happened in such a short time. It seemed a miracle and yet, quite natural that he was there.

His hair was long, not cut the neat army way anymore and he had a beard. Was there still a bit of anti-establishment coursing through his being? Probably, I supposed. I didn't like his long hair, but I didn't like it on

anyone, for that matter. Somehow, though, this was a day when
it wasn't important. My son had earned a certificate in
computer technology, a major accomplishment for someone
who barely squeaked through public schools, hating every
minute of it.

He took his certificate, turned and grinned into my
camera. Ted, Gina, Ria and I clapped and yelled, "Yea,
Casey!" I thought I'd burst with pride.

After all the diplomas had been received and the
ceremony was over we rushed through the crowd to find
Casey. He came toward us, arms outstretched. We clung
to each other and cried happy tears. Ria stayed in the
background away from us. I guess she thought it was a
family moment but, the truth is, she was as much a part
of it as we were because she had been Casey's support
system to stay sober all those months. I wish I had told
her that.

Since his discharge from the army, Casey's life had
changed radically. I learned that when an addict pursues
recovery he must change old habits, old thinking. He
must make new friends, can't go back to the old
drugging and drinking pals. And he must seek new
pastimes. One problem Casey complained about was
boredom. I discussed this with a friend in my writing
class who was a recovering alcoholic, sober five years.

"I don't know what to say to him when he says he's
bored," I told her. "He complains that all he does is go
to work and to school. He says life used to be exciting
when he was drinking and doing drugs. Now he has to
cope with being sober. No fun anymore."

"Tell him to wait it out," my friend said. "After a
while, maybe six more months, it will get easier. Then
it will seem natural to be sober, leading a quieter life.
He'll find excitement in other things. Tell him he's not
alone. We all have the same problem."

She patted my arm in a loving way and I appreciated her more than ever because I realized she had walked the same precarious path as Casey.

I repeated this conversation to him and all he did was shrug his shoulders. This let me know how fragile recovery can be. I didn't press the point. What he needed from us was support, not pressure.

Casey continued going to school and earned his associate degree in October 1991. That graduation ceremony was another joyous occasion. He transferred to the university working toward his B.A. in business management. At one point he said he might even go into drug counseling.

"Time to give back, is that what you're thinking?" I said, trying to mask the surprise I felt.

"I suppose. Doesn't pay much money though. Always wanted to make a million by the time I'm thirty."

This was a family joke and we both laughed. Like most kids he had dreamed of being a millionaire. His ideas for reaching this goal ranged from some great invention to suing anyone who wronged him. "Let's sue!" he'd say at the slightest provocation.

He didn't mention the drug counseling again, so I have no idea what he decided on that score.

"Remember a few days ago when I said I wanted a dog? You'll never guess what happened," Casey said when he called one morning. "On my way to work this morning I saw a puppy on the freeway. He was dodging cars, scared to death. I stopped and a girl in another car stopped and helped me get him into my car."

"He's in your car now at work?" I asked.

"Sure. I finally have my own dog. He's a black Lab. Guess I'll call him Freeway."

That makes sense, I thought. He was so pleased I hated to be a wet blanket about it. He and Gina loved animals. We'd always had a dog, and through the years gerbils, parakeets, and tropical fish. Of course, I was the one taking care of this menagerie. I wasn't sure Casey knew what taking care of a pet entailed. But to my surprise as time passed he and Ria not only had Freeway and her dog, KuzKuz, but two other dogs as well.

Another change in Casey was his interest in taking care of his yard. When he bought a lawn mower and edger I laughed and said, "Well, now you really are part of the establishment."

He chuckled and made no comment.

When he planted morning glories and other flowers in his yard I knew his transition was complete. Home, pets, flowers, and a companion. What more could a mother want?

Well, actually there was one more thing to round out the picture. As a child Casey never could be left to play in his room alone. He had to have someone around at all times. Gina was so different. She'd play in her play pen or room for hours without a whimper, but not Casey. I wished he could be content with himself enough to be alone.

Ria travelled home to Bangor, Maine periodically and Casey was always restless without her. But one night, when she was away, I called him and asked, "How are you doing all alone?"

"The first few days were pretty bad, but now I'm really enjoying myself. I found out that I have to like myself enough to be alone, and I do, for the first time in my life. It's OK. I cook my dinner when I get home from work and go for swims in the ocean. I'm doing just fine."

Hallelujah!

One of Casey's college courses was business law. One night the class met for a session in a small claims court. After the session ended, the judge came out and talked with the class.

I asked Casey if he enjoyed it, and he said, "Yeah, it was

great. The judge was real nice, answered our questions and all. But you know what the best part of the whole thing was? Well, as you know my experiences with courts and judges hasn't been all that great . . . so the best part of last night was that my name wasn't called and I could leave with everyone else!"

In the fall of 1991 I had a disturbing phone call from Casey.

"I'll be over for dinner if it's OK, Mom. I want to go see Karen. She's back on drugs and I want to talk to her a while, see if I can help her. She lives up north of you and I could come by after I see her."

"Do you think that's wise, honey?"

"You mean you think I'll get back on drugs if I see her again."

"No," I said a bit too emphatically. "I have complete faith in you. What I meant is do you think you can be with her and not have the old feelings again?" I was afraid he still loved her.

"I'm over that. Just want to talk to her like I would anyone in trouble. I'm afraid she'll die this time if somebody doesn't stop her." He sounded desperate.

Good and noble were his intentions, I knew. Even so, that didn't keep me from wishing she would leave him alone. She was forever calling him at work. I marvelled at Casey's attitude toward her. Sometimes they would meet and talk for hours. It's hard for me to admit it, but he was far more understanding toward her than I was and I'm usually a kind, forgiving kind of person.

Several hours later he called again and said, "I'm not coming up after all. I called her and all we did was argue. I can't help her . . . I know that now. Hope somebody else can."

Well, of course she would argue, I thought. That's all they ever did when they were married. It was obvious she hadn't changed a bit from her old ways. How could she possibly understand Casey now? He was a different person from the reckless druggie she had known.

What a relief I felt. And deep heart singing gratitude. He had made a wise decision from his head, instead of his heart.

I realized the Serenity Prayer had become a part of him: the serenity to accept the things he could not change, the courage to change the things he could, and the wisdom to know the difference.

* * *

SUB CHAPTER FOURTEEN

The day of my graduation from Coleman, I put on my robe and cap in one of the rooms at school and walked up the ramp to the tent for the ceremony. I couldn't believe all I had done. Dad always fussed at me for never finishing anything I started. But this time I did. And I was proud.

Don't mean to leave Mom out. It's just that there's something different between a father and son, for me anyway. Making him proud of me was still important. Maybe it was all those years when, I guess you can say, I was somewhat of an embarrassment to my folks. Friends of theirs would say how great their kids were doing and there I was on drugs. Not something to brag about.

But now I've changed and so has Dad. He doesn't have to stay awake at night worrying about me, feeling like he's failed.

As I got closer to the ceremony that day, I felt good and confident, but once I saw my family I knew I was going to cry. I was OK until it was over and Mom, Dad, and Gina rushed over to me.

When Dad hugged me it all came rushing out . . . tears and more tears. But that's OK. Crying doesn't bother me anymore.

I went to church with Mom and Dad one Sunday some months later and I could tell how proud they were of me. People would come up and say they had heard everything was going good for me and Dad's eyes were bright and he looked so happy. Cool, huh?

The thing about boredom that Mom mentioned to me has been an important change in my life. Being out there in the world twenty-four hours a day, looking for and scoring drugs, it's a different life. It never stops, never goes to sleep. When the money's there, the drugs are there. It's dependable. Other things are not that way but the drugs can be counted on to be around. It was exciting risking my life getting drugs, maybe getting shot or OD'ing, not knowing if there would be a tomorrow. My motto used to be: eat, drink, and be merry for tomorrow I may die. It was no joke.

That whole life experience stopped when I got sober. Gone. I worked eight hours, slept eight hours, did something else eight hours, and found it hard to adjust to the change. But, somehow, I did it.

So, now I have the life I never thought possible. And it's good. I have tomorrows to think about. Lots of tomorrows.

One of my elective classes at National University was Creative Writing and I had to write some poetry. I wrote this poem. The teacher hated it. But I don't care. It says just what I want to say. I like it.

MY FATHER

A man with conviction and power,
My father.
Successful at life and family,
My father.
There for ones who need,
My father.
There for ones who do not,
My father.
Teaches morality and values,
My father.
Proud, strong, stubborn,
My father.
I love this man,
My father.

* * *

Chapter Fifteen

TED SPEAKS ABOUT HIS OWN U-TURN

THINKING about Casey's life is something like remembering the worst pain ever, but savoring the present because right now is all that is important, right now and what I've learned as a father.

When he was arrested for shoplifting, I really thought it was not all his fault and convinced myself that the humiliation of it might make an indelible imprint on his mind and turn out to be a blessing. I had to wonder why he would do such a dumb thing, if it would make a permanent scar on his mind, and how it would affect his self-esteem. These questions were frustrating because he wouldn't talk to me. I prayed this event would not be the beginning of more trouble and hoped that any punishment from the court would do more good than whatever would come from me. But if I remember correctly his remorse was short-lived.

One particular night I remember all too well. Casey

came home late one night, he was sixteen then, and Anne and I heard him go straight to his room. After a while we heard a loud bang in front of the house. I went outside and found that one of Casey's friends had crashed into his car that was parked out front. I went in to tell Casey and found him sitting on the side of his bed, trying to tie his shoelaces, too drunk to figure out how to do it.

I don't think I have ever felt so sick and disgusted and utterly hopeless. I yelled and screamed at him then went to my room and cried. I could have walked out that night, convinced I had become a total failure as a parent. It took a long time to get that picture of him out of my mind.

The first four or five years after we moved to California were the most frustrating in my entire life. We spent many sleepless nights answering phone calls to get him out of trouble. Nothing I said or did changed anything. He was about as volatile as I, and we almost came to blows a number of times. I'd storm off to another room and he'd leave the house and not come back for days. Then it was hell wondering where he was, wondering when the next phone call would come. It was a nightmare with no waking up for a long time.

I wish I had been like those ideal father's on TV—patient, calm, and wise—but I wasn't. I have a tendency to jump too quickly and it didn't take much for Casey to set me off. Then I'd explode and Casey would react the same way and Anne stood by trying to make peace. No wonder she kept things from me.

One of the worst mistakes I made was to say, "Casey, why did you do such a dumb thing," or "What a stupid thing to do." He thought I was calling him dumb and stupid, but I wasn't. The *things* he did were dumb, not him. Never in all his life has he been dumb.

I recall a movie I saw once: a navy psychiatrist was attempting to calm a patient and the man became violent.

The doctor shouted at him, sending the man cowering to a corner of the room. The doctor rushed over to him and said, "I'm sorry I frightened you but I wasn't yelling at *you*, but at what you were doing!" You see, I had to learn to separate Casey's actions from Casey, because the drugs made him do things he wouldn't have done if he'd been in his own mind. I'm afraid, though, that I was a slow learner where this was concerned.

I remember the story of the '83 Camaro vividly. It pretty well sums up the many experiences with Casey and his "handling" of me, and the inevitable consequences.

His 1976 Chevy was paid for and could have lasted him a long time, but in 1983 he felt he just had to have a better car. I had a friend in the leasing business and we picked out the '83 Camaro because that was what Casey wanted and we could get it for a small down payment. I wanted him to go to college and was willing to do anything I could to convince him, but he didn't want college and preferred to work and have a good car. Before long the sleek charcoal black car looked like a truck. It was dirty, scratched, and worn looking. He had been driving it out in the fields and racing it with his friends. I threatened to take it away from him if he didn't stop. One day he and Karen were home and she had the nerve to say that it was all my fault that Casey was broke because he couldn't afford the car.

We did take it away from him and gave him Anne's car which he wrecked within a week. Then came the motorcycle which he left at home after he enlisted, promising to pay for it. He didn't, of course. History repeated itself over and over.

After he enlisted, I couldn't be sure, but felt his delays in getting accepted were because he still wasn't free of the drugs. Then after he went off to Fort Sill, I was certain the army would make a man of him. For a time we had good reports from him about his progress.

When I learned Karen had joined him it was "here we go again time" in my mind.

For a while after he was transferred to Fort Carson, Colorado, it seemed that we were told just enough good news to give us some hope. During this period I had a degree of false security, thinking everything was going along well but knowing down deep it wasn't. I was proud of him when he told of completing courses and when he had his first promotion. It was a period of little communication until he started calling for money.

My greatest concern was for his health, both before and after the gall bladder operation, afraid he was worse off than he admitted. I wanted to do something but didn't know what, except to pray and I did a lot of that.

When I did find out what was going on, I had a sense of despair and heaviness at not being able to help him, and at the same time was mad as hell that he couldn't or wouldn't straighten out his life. After it was all over he told me there was nothing I could have done or said that would have made a difference.

I never heard the tapes Casey sent to his mother. I couldn't make myself listen to them because I had a hard time accepting all that was happening. When I learned that Casey's sergeant refused to help him, I was ready to get on a plane for Fort Carson and raise hell with everyone there. But my work kept me very busy at the time and kept me from getting too involved. I forced myself to think about other things as much as possible because I just couldn't deal with it.

It looked like a dead-end situation with the dishonorable discharge and the CID business, as if there was no way Casey could come out of it except through a lot of prayer and love. And I think that was when my disgust, anger, and disappointment turned to genuine concern for his life. I'm sure Anne didn't know how many nights I wept remembering my cute, bright little boy. And now look at him, I thought, hoping somehow he could come home and live a normal life.

My joy at having a grandchild was as great as my despair when I found out she really wasn't ours after all. My heart went out to Casey and I wanted to hold him and tell him it wasn't the end of the world and that everything would be all right. Anne and I were both afraid he wouldn't come out of this heartbreak. And again, I prayed. One thing for sure, I felt only disgust toward Karen and did not want her in our home ever again.

When Casey was on his way home, I was ecstatic, and at the same time apprehensive about the future. It was difficult to forget the pain and heartache he had caused his mother and me. There never was a moment when I didn't love him, but many moments when I didn't like him.

He was a pitiful sight when he got off that bus in Oceanside with a duffle bag full of everything he owned, and no money in his pocket. All the love I've ever had went out to him in that early morning hour. He was home and that was all that mattered.

The progress he made was amazing until that one awful slip with the $400 worth of cocaine. Anne called me at work to tell me and I almost lost it. But it was one of the few times I felt strong enough to keep quiet and let him work it out himself.

When he earned his one year token in AA I couldn't have been any more proud if he'd won the Nobel Prize. It was an unbelievable experience. Most of all, Casey has become a real man and a son any father can be proud of. His growth intellectually and practically has been wonderful to see.

Now, when he says, "I love you, Dad," I know he really means it, and I love him.

* * *

Chapter Sixteen

IN the fall of 1991 Casey's employer initiated security clearance for him, and on October 15 it was denied. Casey appealed the decision, and on October 28 requested a hearing before an administrative judge. The hearing was held on January 27, 1992. During the hearing seven Government documents and Casey's testimony were admitted into evidence.

Quoting from the transcript: "Applicant was a long term poly-substance abuser, of both drugs and alcohol, who, supposedly since June 16, 1989, has been abstinent. His substance abuse resulted in one alcohol-related arrest, on July 31, 1988, when he was twenty-three years old; hospitalization and treatment on November 14, 1988, for a drug overdose, which was a result of 'free-basing' cocaine: non-judicial punishment under Article 15, Uniform Code of Military Justice, for wrongful use of cocaine, on November 15, 1988; and an administrative discharge from the United States Army, on April 28, 1989, for misconduct involving the use of illegal drugs. He was issued a General Discharge certificate. Applicant was originally recommended for a discharge characterization of Under Other Than Honorable Conditions. However, based on his productive participation with Army CID authorities, while serving as a 'narc' in a drug investigation at his military post, that recommendation was upgraded."

The transcript listed all of Casey's and Karen's crimes for obtaining drug money and reported their petition for bankruptcy and subsequent discharge of debts totaling $29,888.15 in October 1989.

The transcript further states: " . . . from 1977, when he was twelve years old, to June 1989, he abused alcohol as well as illegal substances . . . to the point of intoxication and blackouts; occasionally used amphetamines, 1980-81; used marijuana, about twenty-five times during 1981-89; used crystal methamphetamine, about two times a year, during 1983-89; used cocaine and 'crack' cocaine from one time a month to as frequently as daily, during 1983-June 1989; experimented with heroin once in about 1985; used psilocybin mushrooms, about ten times, during 1987-89; and used lysergic acid diethylamide (LSD), about twenty times, during 1988-89. During basic training he abstained from all drug abuse.—When (he) was finally discharged from the army in April 1989, he felt that his life had hit bottom. It was either 'quit or die!'. He chose to quit."

The transcript continues to recite Casey's entrance into AA, his excellent work record, and pursuance of college education.

The application for security clearance had been denied since Casey had not been sober for the required three year period. The judge further stated: " . . . after plummeting to the bottom of the abyss, he has abstained for at least two years and seven months . . . He has overcome tremendous obstacles to arrive at the point in which he is now. However, Applicant has faced and conquered his prob-

lems, and been candid about them, and I do not believe that
any useful purpose would be served at this point to hold his
feet to the fire for a greater period of time simply to comply
with the cold letter of the adjudication policy guidelines . . .
now that he is no longer looking at life through the bottom of
an alcohol bottle, or through the haze of the wafting smoke
of an abused illegal substance, Applicant has attempted to
resolve the matter . . . he has finally pulled himself together,
cleaned the slate, and dedicated himself to positive action .
. . he learned and grew from those experiences and his con-
duct changed for the better."

The clearance was granted.

Casey continued his education toward a BA degree in
business management, working full time and going to
school at night. The sum he owed on student loans continued to grow. This prompted him to file an appeal with
The Department of the Army Appeals Division to upgrade
his discharge and reinstate his benefits for GI Bill education rights and the ability to seek a GI loan for a home.
The transcript quoted was included in his appeal. No re-
sponse to the appeal was ever received.

During the summer of 1992 Karen left Lisa with her
parents to live her life on the Oceanside streets. I don't
know where she is now. Joyce and Bill went their separate
ways. Bill remains clean and sober, leading a productive
life. Sadly, Joyce returned to her old ways and came to
Casey for help once. He was upset by the encounter and,
feeling she wasn't sincere, didn't want to see her anymore.

Our world seemed bleak when Karen took Lisa out of
our lives. Yet, through a tiny crack in the window of my
deepest sanguine hopes, I glimpsed a time when we might
have other grandchildren. On October 1, 1991, our family,
including Ria, witnessed the birth of Gina's son, Jonathan.
Never was any child more cherished.

An experience I had one afternoon haunted me for

days. I was doing errands and stopped at a Target store. As I approached the entrance, a girl in ragged jeans dashed out of the store toward me. A man in hot pursuit, grabbed her black tote bag, knocking her down on the concrete walk.

"Give me that!" he shouted.

"Let go, you bastard," she yelled back.

While they struggled for the bag, a young boy came between them, freeing the girl. "Get outa here," he said. The girl jumped up, grabbed her bag, and ran toward an old orange van.

Another man rushed out of the store, tackled the boy, and turned, watching the girl. "Hurry, somebody get the license number." The other security guard raced after the van, staring at the license plate, which he jotted down on a note pad.

The boy lay face down on the concrete, while the men handcuffed him. "I didn't know she took anything, I didn't know," he cried out. "Oh, God, let me go, please let me go."

The men yanked him to his feet. Dirty streaks of tears rolled down his round face. His dark eyes were wild and frightened.

After they disappeared into the store, I stared down at my clenched fists. Tears dimmed my eyes and my stomach churned with a sick feeling of more emotions than I can name. Was it like that when Casey was arrested at a Target store in Tulsa so many years ago? Did he cry out the same way? If he did I hoped someone was there to feel what I felt. It was a mixture of compassion for the boy, anger at the girl for deserting him, and frustration at their need to steal. I had no doubt the craving for drugs was at the root of it.

Whatever the reason, I realized something that day. When I gazed into the poor boy's eyes, I understood my son. I glimpsed the boy's confusion, his need, and his inability to help himself, and instinctively, I loved him.

One morning on my way to work, long before Gina and Casey were born during those early years when I ached for a child, a program on the radio caught my attention. Mothers were talking about the wonder and joy of motherhood. In the midst of uncontrollable tears, I cried out, "Oh, dear God, will I ever know what it's like?" A promise rang back in the stillness of the car, "I will give you more." It was as clear to me as a real voice. And I have been given more, perhaps more to cope with in the world's eyes, but far more lasting lessons than just coping. I learned to love unconditionally. The greatest part of it all was seeing Casey and his father finally come together. The love and understanding and respect they learned for each other make every agonizing moment of those trying years worthwhile.

Many times, in my volunteer work, sitting face to face with inmates in prison visiting rooms, I looked into their troubled eyes. And when I told them, with all the conviction I could muster, that if they don't believe anything else in this world they can know that God loves them right where they are, right as they are, then a visible change takes place. I've seen tough, burly, battle scarred men weep unashamed while we look quietly into each others' hearts.

During the sometimes hopeless years of Casey's youth, I often wondered why I had been so determined to be a mother. I never doubted about Gina, but at times, I thought it might have been better for Casey if someone else had adopted him, someone who could have understood him better and been more help to him. Now, remembering all the joys, Ted and I are filled with unspeakable gratitude. We wouldn't have missed having him in our lives for anything in this world.

* * *

Chapter Seventeen

DURING the years involved in writing this story, I sometimes wondered if anything could have been more trying than dealing with Casey's struggles and ordeals. Now I know that we do what we are compelled to do one step at a time, one day at a time. One can either sink down into the mire or resolve to overcome whatever happens. The rest of Casey's story forced Ted and me to accept something no parent should ever have to face.

During the next five years of Casey's sobriety, he accomplished more than we had ever dreamed for him, and I think I became so involved in his triumphs that I didn't notice anything else going on in his life. Ted did and sometimes voiced his suspicions, but I went right on in my own little world.

My brother passed away in May 1994 leaving quite a nice inheritance to be divided between Gina, Casey, and me. Casey decided to buy a small house in Imperial Beach. At that point he was nearing the time when he would soon graduate from National University with a BA in Business Management. His student loan total was around $30,000 at that time and the University required him to go ahead and enroll for all his Masters degree classes, which he did.

Earlier that year his manager promoted him to Senior Planner, giving him more responsibility and, of course, a raise in pay.

Casey moved into his new house and seemed content. Everything looked perfect, but a few things in his life were not. He met a fellow named Charlie on the beach and brought him home with him to sober him up. Charlie didn't like Ria and somehow brought friction between her and Casey, then Casey began an affair with another girl causing matters to become worse and worse.

A week or two before Christmas, Ria decided to spend the holidays with her mother in Bangor, Maine, hoping to work things out when she returned.

The Sunday before Christmas, Casey met us for lunch after church. He seemed quieter than usual but not depressed and, I'll admit, I didn't really give his mood much thought. He called on Thursday to say he was sick and had stayed home from work that day. Friday he called around five-thirty after getting home from work. "It's been a long day," he said, and I could hear the weariness in his voice.

"Are you feeling all right?" I asked.

"Better, but not great. I'm just going to crash in my room and go to bed early. I'll go Christmas shopping to-morrow and call you during the half-time of the Cowboys game so we can plan where we'll eat dinner."

He knew his dad would be watching the Dallas Cow-boys game, our old home team. As to the dinner plans, our family had been eating out on Christmas Eve for years. Most of the time it was an adventure just to find a place open and we'd end up eating at Denny's or some hamburger place. The place didn't matter—we were together.

We talked a bit longer, then I said bye to my son and hung up the phone.

Christmas Eve day was filled with the usual activities. We had decided to spend Christmas at home with Casey and not make the trip again to Chandler, Arizona, where Gina lived with her husband, Mark, and three year-old Jonathan. So most of the day was spent missing my daughter, and at the same time looking forward to the evening with Casey and Christmas day, when he and Ted and I would all be together.

Around four in the afternoon, the telephone rang. Ted answered and I heard him say, "Yes, I'm sitting down."

A short silence then he almost screamed, handing me the phone. "Casey's dead," he moaned. He paced the floor behind my chair saying it couldn't be and that he didn't want to live anymore.

Suddenly everything seemed to be in slow motion and unreal. Listening to Ted's agony I had to somehow remain sane. He handed me the phone and after I said hello I found out it was Charlie, the one Casey took into his home to sober up. I struggled with all the strength I had to ask Charlie what had happened.

"Well, he came home last night and went to his room. Didn't even eat anything that I know of. He had told me to let him sleep today, but when he didn't come out by one-thirty or so, I went in there and found him. I called 911. They're here now."

To myself I wondered why he had waited so long that morning to go into Casey's room. I also wondered why he didn't call *us* right away after calling 911.

A long silence then Charlie said, "The investigator wants to talk to you."

"Ma'am," he said, then asked me some questions I can't recall. "It appears he's OD'd but the coroner will have to determine the cause and let you know."

We spoke some more but I simply don't remember the rest. Charlie came back on the line and said, "I found a plate with a spoon, a syringe, and some coke and heroin on it in the floor of the closet. He bought the stuff down on the beach on his way home yesterday."

He what, I screamed to myself? And why? After being sober five years, why would he do such a stupid thing?

The rest of the night remains in a fog. Ted and I decided not to call Gina until the next afternoon, to let them enjoy their first Christmas together before telling them.

Early the next morning, Ted and I drove down to Casey's house. Charlie was there but left soon after we arrived. One of the first things I saw when we entered the house was the framed cross stitch I'd given to Casey, "God grant me the serenity to accept the things I cannot change, the courage to change the things I can, and the wisdom to know the difference." This prayer hangs on the wall behind my computer desk where I'm now writing.

Seeing his clothes in the closet, his shoes, his books, his watch, and first year AA token laying about his room without him, all remain in my memory. Just things, yet a part of him. But his presence still was felt, his smile, and warm hugs.

I called Ria after we got back home, and she said Charlie had already called her, and with cruelty in his voice said, "Well, you'll never come back to this house again because he's dead." She also told us that Casey had called her that Friday before Christmas Eve and asked her to come home and marry him. So why, I thought, would he buy drugs and OD?

She wanted to come home to Casey's house, but we felt it was best for her to stay with her mother and promised to send her things to her.

During one of the trips down to Casey's house, the next door neighbor spoke to us out in the yard and said he'd heard strange cries coming from the house that night. We tried to press him further but that was all he would say.

In the clear light of the days that followed, we questioned Charlie further. His hatred and resentment toward Ria and things he'd said about what happened that night changed from time to time. I called the police officer who had answered the 911 call and asked her to go back to the house and look for anything that might suggest foul play, perhaps talk to the neighbor next door about what he'd heard. She promised to call me the next day, but didn't. When I called the precinct, I was told she'd been transferred to another department and they wouldn't tell me where. Too many unanswered questions remained, too many things that didn't make sense.

Charlie stayed on at the house for a short time and helped me pack Ria's things to mail to her. Then one day he suddenly left taking Ria's bicycle with him, one Casey had bought for her. I traced him to his sister's house, had several conversations with him, and asked him to return the bicycle. After a while, he wouldn't return my calls and finally disappeared. No one would help us. Doors were slamming in our faces. I wanted to scream but who would hear?

One afternoon about a week after Casey passed on, two of the people Casey worked for came to the house. They talked on and on about Casey's work, how dedicated he was, how bright, good humored, and well liked. One of them said that as Senior Planner, Casey was responsible for seeing all the jobs through to completion and he was never bashful about going to the "big boss" to push things along. They both agreed this was a quality the "big boss" appreciated. I don't believe Ted and I had ever been more grateful and proud of our son.

Before they left one of them handed us a video they had made to show their appreciation for Casey. It took several days to gather our courage to watch it, but when we finally did this was what we saw and heard: it began as if Casey was arriving for work, the car going up the long drive then parking in his spot in back of the offices. The camera showed only the path taken as the driver got out of the car and walked to the door of the receiving department. At that moment a man across the lot called out, "Hey, Casey, how's it going?" It was as if Casey were really there.

Once inside the offices, one after another of Casey's co-workers told about experiences they'd had with him, how he joked with everyone, how friendly and helpful he was. Ted and I held hands and cried, but it was a nice cry, if there is such a thing.

The autopsy report came about two weeks later. "Accidental overdose" it said. The ME said Casey's system had been drug free too long to handle the shock of both drugs: cocaine an upper, and heroin a downer, which he'd told me he never really enjoyed taking. End of story on paper. But was it?

Too many whys. Why would Casey call Ria and ask her to marry him then take two drugs that fight with each other to such a lethal degree? Didn't he know what a chance he was taking? He had a new house that he was proud of, a job he enjoyed, and college work about to enter into a new final phase. And out in his back yard was a new chow puppy he adored. None of it made sense, but then a sudden death rarely does.

I was so frustrated and felt I had to do something to find answers, but what else could I do? The awful fact remained that Casey was gone and all the answers in the world wouldn't bring him back. If Charlie had anything to do with Casey's death, I would have to leave him to God's justice for no one goes unpunished forever, if not here then at least in the hereafter. This reasoning was the only way I have been able to let the struggle go, although sometimes, in the quiet of the night, I still yearn to know what really happened and have to let it go all over again.

Of course, now I admit Ted was right to be cautious about Casey. It was apparent from the beer in his refrigerator he'd gone back to some of his old ways, maybe not to the past extremes, and we suspected that Ria was also drinking again. Maybe the beer was hers, not Casey's. Nothing confirmed, only nagging suspicions.

Maybe it was better not to know the truth. Ted was convinced that Casey simply couldn't handle the sudden supply of money—the inheritance from my brother and his raise in pay—and buying a house. Maybe he suddenly felt too comfortable. So many maybes.

I can't speak for Ted but what did I learn through all this chaos? What "advice" would I give to someone else going through the same problem with a loved one? I suppose first on the list would be to keep a close watch on the individual for any signs of restlessness or change in attitude. Be alert to mood swings, and never, ever take recovery for granted.

Someone once remarked there is nothing so devastating as the loss of a child. All those years of promise gone, years when the child should be going forward long past the parent's lifetime. But Ted and I have to rely on our faith in God to sustain us, knowing that our child is free now, going right on in a safe yet distant place, learning to deal with his old demons and temptations in a different way.

It's like visualizing a sea gull drifting on the breeze over a rough sea, then quite unexpectedly he leaves his companions and circles higher and higher beyond the clouds, his strong white wings outspread, until he becomes a tiny speck. Finally he disappears from sight into the far reaches of the sky, beyond the blue horizon.

But has he ceased to be? No, I don't believe so. All that we identified with him—life, intelligence, vitality, humor, and warmth—still remains in our hearts. We must accept the fact we won't see him any more in this world, but we know he is finally free as he continues on his way, still learning, and progressively ascending all the time.

* * * *

Go To Hell and Make a U-Turn